STEFON DIGGS

by
Doug Olson, Jr.

Minneapolis, Minnesota

Dedication
For Doug Olson. For Believing. For Encouraging. For Being my Dad. Thank You. —"Little Dougie"

Acknowledgments
The author would like to thank Natalie Fowler for her invaluable research and Jen Imsdahl for her article suggestion; Jessica Freeburg for throwing my name into the hat for this project and Ryan Jacobson for taking the chance on me; Doug Olson to whom this book is dedicated; and, of course, my wife and children, who support my aspirations and give me the time and space to find my own end zone with only a minor amount of sarcasm.

Edited by Ryan Jacobson
Proofread by Emily Beaumont and Cheri Jacobson
Cover design by Ryan Jacobson and germancreative

Stefon Diggs photograph (front) by Greg Trott. Copyright 2019 The Associated Press. Football image (back cover) copyright David Lee / Shutterstock.com. For additional photography credits, see page 111.

The information presented here is accurate to the best of our knowledge. However, the information is not guaranteed. It is solely the reader's responsibility to verify the information before relying upon it.

This book is not affiliated with, authorized, endorsed, or sponsored by the National Football League, its players, or anyone involved with the league.

The use of any trademarks is for identification and reference purposes only and does not imply any association with the trademark holder.

TABLE OF CONTENTS

PROLOGUE

Stefon Diggs found his spot on the right side of the football field. Wide receiver Adam Thielen was wide to the left side, and quarterback Case Keenum stood, waiting to begin the play. The crowd rumbled, hoping for a miracle, but Stefon barely heard them. He was focused on one goal.

It was January 14, 2018, and the Minnesota Vikings were seconds away from the end of their season. A loss would knock them out of the playoffs. They built a 17–0 lead by halftime, but that lead had dwindled away. The New Orleans Saints now led, 24–23, with just 10 seconds remaining in the game. Minnesota possessed the ball, but they were 61 yards from the end zone.

According to ESPN, the Vikings had just a 2.6 percent chance of winning the game.

The play was called "Gun Buffalo Right Key Left Seven Heaven." Keenum operated out of the shotgun position— the "Gun"—5 yards behind the center. Three receivers (including Stefon) were bunched on the right side, or "Buffalo Right." "Key Left" was Keenum's intention to target the left wide receiver: Thielen. "Seven" called for a deep route down the sideline. The "Heaven" part came from the hope that good things would happen.

The intent behind the play was simple: Get the ball down the field and get out of bounds. That would stop the clock so that kicker Kai Forbath could attempt a game-winning field goal.

As Stefon knew quite well, things didn't always go as planned. This was going to be hard, but it wasn't the hardest thing he had ever done.

Sixty-one yards. Ten seconds.

This was possible.

Anything was possible.

Stefon caught 6 passes for 137 yards against the Saints.

1

⟨⟨⟨⟨ TOUGH COACH ⟩⟩⟩⟩

Stefon Mar'Sean Diggs was born on November 29, 1993, in Gaithersburg, Maryland. He was the first child of Stephanie and Aron (pronounced "A-Ron") Diggs. Mrs. Diggs was 27 when Stefon was born, and Mr. Diggs was 25. Four years later, another child joined the family. Stefon's younger brother, Trevon, was born in 1997.

The family tree also included Stefon's half-brother and half-sister: Aron, Jr., was 4 years older than Stefon, and Porsche was 3 years older.

Stefon loved football from the moment he discovered the sport. He spent countless hours racing around the house with a football in his hands. He attended his half-brother Aron's games and knew, even at a young age, that he wanted to play the exciting game.

In the summer of 1999, Stefon asked to play in the local football program for 6-year-olds: the Montgomery County Youth Football League. His parents agreed, and Mr. Diggs took it upon himself to become the workout coach for Stefon and Trevon. He also became a coach of Stefon's team, along with Garrett King.

Mr. Diggs loved football, but he had spent much of his youth primarily as a basketball player.

Stefon's father was well over 6 feet tall and weighed close to 250 pounds. So he was an imposing figure, and he proved to be a harsh coach. He rarely spoke in positive terms and chose to raise his children with "tough love." He believed that life wasn't easy, so his kids' lives shouldn't be either. During workouts, if one of the children got tired or fell down, Mr. Diggs would tell them to stop crying, get up, and go again.

Stefon and Trevon didn't know many other kids in the neighborhood. Their lives were school, football, training with their dad, and little else.

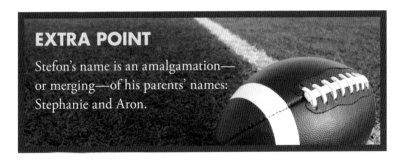

EXTRA POINT

Stefon's name is an amalgamation—or merging—of his parents' names: Stephanie and Aron.

Mrs. Diggs didn't agree with her husband's approach. She often asked him to slow down, give the kids a break, and allow them to be children. It seemed as if her husband was pushing his kids too hard to be what he wanted them to be. That wasn't the case. He was pushing them to be what they wanted to be. He was pushing them to always strive for more, to become better than they currently were, in anything they did.

Coach King's wife agreed with Stefon's mom. She pleaded with her husband to talk to Mr. Diggs. But Coach King saw his fellow coach as fair. Mr. Diggs was hard on the players, but he rewarded them too—sometimes spending his own money to buy them things.

A lesson Mr. Diggs worked hard to teach was that achievement came from a competitive attitude. This, to him, was more important than encouraging words and pats on the back.

Stefon did not mind his father's coaching style. He knew that it would make him better, stronger, and more determined to succeed.

The young player got more than a winning attitude from his pops. Stefon inherited large hands. His hands were so big that they embarrassed him. He kept them hidden in his pockets as often as he could.

By the time he was 10 years old, Stefon realized that his large hands were a gift. They helped him to become an excellent pass catcher, even at a young age.

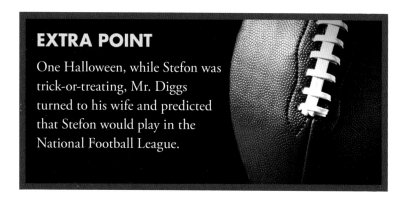

EXTRA POINT

One Halloween, while Stefon was trick-or-treating, Mr. Diggs turned to his wife and predicted that Stefon would play in the National Football League.

2

⪦⪧⪦⪧ RESPONSIBILITIES ⪦⪧⪦⪧

When Stefon was 11 years old, he participated in the Montgomery County Youth Football championship game. Mr. Diggs still coached his son's team, the Montgomery Village Chiefs. He called for Stefon to run the ball on a fourth-down play. The ball was snapped, and Stefon took the handoff. He burst through the defensive line. Then he lowered his shoulder, and he rammed into an opposing player before falling to the ground.

The play gained enough for a first down.

Stefon turned to his father. A wide smile spread across Mr. Diggs' face. It was the first time Stefon remembered receiving praise on the football field from his pops, and it was much clearer than words could have been. Mr. Diggs was proud, and so was his son.

By then, Stefon had made a lasting impression in the area. He had excelled as a quarterback, then as a running back, before settling in at the wide receiver position. Private high schools in Maryland and nearby Washington, D.C., were eyeing the young athlete—with hopes of recruiting him to one day play for their team.

Mr. Diggs was partial to Our Lady of Good Counsel (OLGC), a Catholic school in nearby Olney, Maryland.

Mr. Diggs wasn't the only person who wanted Stefon to enroll there. Bob Milloy, the football coach at OLGC, saw Stefon play in 7th grade and began heavily recruiting him.

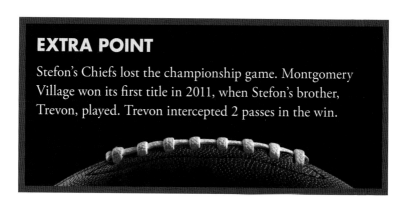

EXTRA POINT

Stefon's Chiefs lost the championship game. Montgomery Village won its first title in 2011, when Stefon's brother, Trevon, played. Trevon intercepted 2 passes in the win.

Before choosing a high school, Stefon still had 2 years of middle school to go. There was plenty of work to do and things to learn—on and off the field. Stefon had time.

Mr. Diggs, unfortunately, did not. He was diagnosed with a serious disease known as Congestive Heart Failure (CHF). The condition generally developed when the heart couldn't pump enough blood throughout the body. It was a progressive disease that grew worse over time, and it was hard to treat.

Mr. Diggs remained a presence on the field for as long as he could, even though CHF sapped his energy. He coached his sons and his team from a chair on the sidelines.

Eventually, his illness led to several trips to the hospital. Even from a hospital bed, he did not forget about his boys, often asking his wife for game updates.

With his dad's health failing, Stefon became a sort of "father figure" to his younger brother. Trevon looked up to him, and Stefon recognized the importance of setting a good example. Whether it was a natural part of his character or a learned behavior, Stefon became the person his father always wanted him to be.

When Stefon was 13, his dad took him for a drive. Stefon noticed a new pair of shoes, but they were too small for him. Stefon and his father traveled together to an unfamiliar place, where a tremendous surprise awaited.

Mr. Diggs introduced Stefon to an 11-year-old boy. This was Mar'Sean, Stefon's younger half-brother. The shoes

Stefon was recruited by Our Lady of Good Counsel High School.

were for Mar'Sean—and Stefon suddenly had another family member to care for. The two brothers got along right away and quickly developed a close relationship.

With Mr. Diggs' continued trips to the hospital, there wasn't always money left for things the family needed—like food. The children had to get creative at meal time. Sometimes, Stefon would split syrup sandwiches with his siblings.

Along with school, football, and training, Stefon added a new task to his daily routine: visiting his father. Every day, he left practice and went straight to the hospital. When necessary, Stefon cut and combed his father's hair. He put a watch on his father's wrist, knowing that Pops always wanted to look presentable.

He didn't mind doing any of this. His father would be back home again soon. He would always come back home.

Wouldn't he?

3

⟨⟨⟨⟨ GOODBYE ⟩⟩⟩⟩

Trevon was already asleep when the boys' father came into the bedroom. Stefon remained awake. He sat up in his bed. His father took a seat across from him. Pops had news. He was going back to the hospital once more. This time was the last; he would not be coming back.

Stefon didn't argue. He could tell that it was the truth. Despite knowing that his father would not approve, Stefon began to cry.

Mr. Diggs told him there was nothing to cry about. No amount of tears would change the situation. Yet when Stefon lifted his eyes, he saw that his dad was crying too.

In that bedroom, with tears on both of their faces, the father tasked his son with the duties of an adult. "Take care of your mother and brothers. Look to their needs. Teach your brothers to do the right thing. Work hard. And always, always, get up and keep going."

Stefon's dad returned to the hospital. Just as he had predicted, his health worsened. This time, it did not improve. Soon, he was no longer able to live and breathe on his own. Special "life support" machines were hooked up to him to keep him alive, for a time.

On January 16, 2008, Stefon and the rest of his family gathered together in that hospital room. They sadly and quietly watched together as doctors removed the machines that were keeping Pops alive.

With life support no longer regulating his heartbeat, Mr. Aron Diggs passed away. He was 39 years old.

4

NEW BEGINNINGS

There had been plenty of people crying after the passing of his father, but Stefon was not one of them. He grieved. He missed the man. He sometimes felt as if he'd lost everything. But he still had the rest of his family, he still had school, and he still had football.

His mindset changed. It had to change, in order to honor his father's wishes. He'd been given a duty, a hard burden for a 14-year-old boy to shoulder. But he intended to live up to it.

Fortunately for Stefon, a great part of his strength came from his mother. She spent most of her adult life working as a service attendant at Amtrak, a railroad company. She continued to do so, even as she suddenly found herself raising three boys alone. She could get tough when she needed to. Even as the boys grew older and bigger, she got after them and kept them in line.

Mrs. Diggs had always preferred basketball. She left football to her husband, and he had set the boys on the right path. She knew very little about football. But it was important to the boys. Now, with her husband gone, it became important to her. Like her oldest son, she would rise to the challenge.

She began reading about the sport, including the all-important recruiting process. This would serve Stefon and his brothers well in the future.

EXTRA POINT

Stefon attributes his courage to his mother. He even nick-named her "Superwoman."

Coach Bob Milloy from Our Lady of Good Counsel High School continued to recruit Stefon to play for his team. Milloy was a legendary coach. In fact, he had more wins than any other football coach in Maryland. Milloy was also an excellent recruiter, and Stefon was easy to convince. The boy wanted to honor his father's wishes, so he chose to attend OLGC as a freshman in 2008.

The team was already loaded with talent—including future college and National Football League (NFL) players, like safety Blake Countess. Stefon still managed to stand out. He saw playing time on offense and on defense, and he truly excelled on special teams as a punt returner.

The OLGC Falcons were such a good team that college recruiters attended their practices. One day, Stefon made an amazing one-handed catch. An assistant coach from the University of Maryland was quite impressed. He offered Stefon a scholarship to play for them in 4 years!

When Stefon got home, he cried tears of joy. He wasn't sure if he would choose the University of Maryland—but he knew that he could play football in college some day.

The Falcons rolled through the season, dominating every opponent on their way to an 11–0 record. Their only loss of the season came against the DeMatha Stags, 34–7, in the Washington Catholic Athletic Conference (WCAC) Football Championship.

After his freshman season, Stefon was named to the WCAC All-Conference first team, as a specialist, for his outstanding play on special teams.

Over the coming months, he began to receive scholarship offers from other colleges—Pittsburgh, Miami, and more—even though he still had 3 more years of high school to go.

Expectations soared for Stefon's sophomore season. The youngster played running back and was touted as one of the best players in the conference. As for his team, the Falcons had hopes of winning the championship in 2009. After all, they had played in the title game for 5 straight years—and lost all 5 times to DeMatha.

The season got off to a solid start. OLGC won the first two games by a combined score of 70–16.

When the Gilman Greyhounds visited the Falcons on September 17, Stefon played another fantastic game.

The Falcons jumped to a 14–3 lead in the first quarter. Stefon helped his team extend that lead in the second quarter. OLGC went into halftime ahead, 35–18. Gilman

Stefon electrified fans with his ability to run with the football.

outscored the Falcons in the second half, but they couldn't contain Stefon. The Greyhounds fell, 49–37.

Stefon finished with 5 rushing attempts for 51 yards and a rushing touchdown. More impressively, he returned 2 kickoffs for 2 touchdowns—one for 94 yards and another for 87.

The Falcons continued their winning ways and built a record of 5–0 when DeMatha hosted them. For Stefon's team, it was a chance to avenge last season's only loss.

Through three quarters of play, the Falcons dominated on both sides of the ball. The visiting team worked to a 21–3 lead. But in the fourth quarter, DeMatha running back

Marcus Coker exploded for 3 rushing touchdowns. The Stags rallied from behind to steal the win, 24–21.

Stefon and his teammates would not forget the bitter taste of defeat; they would not lose again. They reeled off five more wins en route to another WCAC championship game—and another rematch with DeMatha.

The evenly matched teams battled to a 7–7 tie in the fourth quarter. With less than 11 minutes to go, the Falcons took the lead on a 20-yard touchdown pass. It was all that OLGC needed. They won the game—and their first ever WCAC championship—by a score of 14–7.

5

⟨⟨⟨⟨⟨ MOST OUTSTANDING ⟩⟩⟩⟩⟩

Stefon was a star player and a champion. But even after 2 years at OLGC, he struggled as a student. His teachers—and assistant principal Patt Perfetto in particular—saw Stefon as smart with plenty of potential. But Stefon didn't seem to take his classes seriously.

Still, he was popular and friendly. Even if he lacked a certain level of maturity and responsibility, he was kind to everyone. As Stefon entered his junior year in 2010, his teachers and coaches wished that he would work as hard in the classroom as he did on the football field.

As the reigning WCAC champions, the Falcons were a target for other teams. Everyone wanted to defeat them, to knock them off their throne. But Stefon and his teammates were ready to play.

Our Lady of Good Counsel won their first matchup, but they were trounced by the Gilman Greyhounds a week later. The Falcons bounced back with a three-game winning streak before familiar foe DeMatha handed them their second loss of the season, 31–28.

After that frustrating game, Stefon and his teammates pulled together to win another five games on their way to the championship. Yet again, their opponent would be the DeMatha Stags.

The game was played at Navy-Marine Corps Stadium in Annapolis on November 21. Falcons quarterback Zach Dancel starred from the outset. He rushed for the game's first touchdown near the end of the first quarter.

In the second quarter, Dancel connected with Stefon on a short screen pass at the 50-yard line. The speedy junior took over from there. Stefon showed off his speed and skill as he took the pass all the way to the end zone.

Later in the quarter, Dancel and Stefon connected for another touchdown, this time from 30 yards out. At halftime, OLGC led, 21–3.

The score grew even more lopsided in the second half. The Falcons added three touchdowns to their total, including a third touchdown pass from Dancel to Stefon.

When all was said and done, the Falcons routed the Stags, 42–3. They were once again champions of the Washington Catholic Athletic Conference.

As a junior, Stefon racked up 810 receiving yards, and he scored 23 touchdowns. He was among the top players in the state. In fact, he was runner-up for the Gatorade Maryland Player of the Year, behind future NFL wide receiver Darius Jennings.

Stefon was also recognized as one of the most talented players in the country when he was invited to attend the U.S. Army All-American Junior Combine. The event showcased the athleticism of underclassmen to college coaches and scouts.

For the event, Stefon traveled to San Antonio, Texas, in January 2011. He performed well in drills that measured his physical ability, such as the 40-yard dash and the vertical jump. But Stefon truly stood out in one-on-one drills. Many of the best defensive backs from high schools across the country tried to cover him. None of them could.

Stefon was so impressive that he received the award as the Rivals.com Most Outstanding Performer.

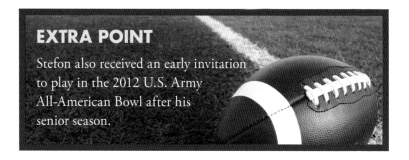

EXTRA POINT

Stefon also received an early invitation to play in the 2012 U.S. Army All-American Bowl after his senior season.

The young running back and wide receiver proved himself as an elite football player. So it came as no surprise that college offers continued to come his way. He still wasn't sure where he wanted to attend college, but Stefon expressed interest in Florida State, Miami, South Carolina, and Virginia Tech.

He still had time—more than a year to decide. No one knew what the future would bring. Not even Stefon.

6

CSSSSS HOMETOWN HERO SSSSSS

Football was not Stefon's only high school sport. He also participated in track and field. He ran the 100-meter dash and the 200-meter dash. He took part in relay races, too, in which each of four runners ran part of the race.

Of course, football remained his primary focus. But during his junior year, he also awakened to the importance of his education. He realized that it would be an essential part of his future—both in college and beyond. Plus, he needed to set a better example for his brothers.

Stefon began working hard at studying and improving his effort in school. He set a goal for himself to get all "A" and "B" grades through his senior year.

Heading into his final football season, Stefon achieved a type of celebrity status. Although Stefon didn't seem to be aware of it, his coaches were. They told Stefon that even elementary-aged kids would start emulating him when they played. Fans would all want Stefon's autograph on footballs, shirts, gloves, anything they could get.

Stefon scoffed at the idea. He was only doing what he loved to do: play a game. He was not a celebrity.

One night, he saw a group of children standing outside the fence behind the Falcons' end zone. They pleaded for autographs and souvenirs. Stefon suddenly understood. He was more than just a 17-year-old boy. He was an inspiration and a role model—to his brothers and even to people he had never met.

Most people knew Stefon as a standout on offense. But he was a stellar cornerback on defense too. His goal was to do everything he could to bring home one more WCAC championship in 2011.

The Falcons were tested in their first game, against the Manatee Hurricanes, one of the best teams in the country. OLGC scored the only touchdown of the first half. Manatee tied the game, 7–7, in the third quarter.

OLGC answered. With the ball at the 20-yard line, Stefon ran a deep route down the left side of the field and found an opening in the defense. Quarterback Brendan Marshall heaved the ball to him. Stefon hauled it in, angled to his right, and raced to the right corner of the end zone for an 80-yard score.

The Hurricanes tied the game again in the fourth quarter, and then OLGC reclaimed the lead with a field goal. But Manatee put together a last-minute drive to tie the game again with just 3 seconds left in regulation.

The 17–17 tie meant that the game would be decided in overtime. Neither team managed to score in the first overtime, so the contest extended into a second overtime.

With the game on the line, the Falcons called a play for Stefon. Marshall took the snap at Manatee's 25-yard line and rolled to his right. He lofted the football to the

Stefon's speed made him a threat to catch passes deep downfield.

back corner of the end zone. Wide open, Stefon caught the pass, tapped his feet in bounds, then rolled out of the end zone.

Touchdown!

The play was enough to give OLGC a hard-fought victory. Stefon finished the game with 6 catches for 131 yards and 2 scores.

In the weeks that followed, the Falcons continued to win, and Stefon continued to perform. He caught 6 passes for 101 yards and 3 touchdowns against Gonzaga. A week later, he hauled in 4 receptions for 125 yards versus Red Lion Christian Academy.

OLGC won every game on their schedule and reached the WCAC championship game undefeated. This time, a different opponent awaited: the Gonzaga Eagles. An 8–3 team, Gonzaga had knocked DeMatha out of the playoffs a week earlier, 28–27.

Stefon set the tone for his final game as a Falcon. On the first offensive play of the day, he scored on a 70-yard run down the left sideline.

From there, things only got better for the defending champs. The underdog Eagles fumbled away the football 3 times and threw 2 interceptions. Stefon and his team jumped to a 35–0 lead at halftime and ultimately won the game, 42–0.

The victory capped a perfect 12–0 season, the first undefeated football season in school history. For the third straight year, the Falcons were WCAC champions.

EXTRA POINT

Stefon grew up less than an hour from Washington, D.C., so his family cheered for the Redskins. But Stefon's favorite NFL team was the Dallas Cowboys.

Throughout the 2011 season, teams that played OLGC always planned for ways to stop Stefon. To counteract this, Coach Milloy came up with at least two new ways each week to get Stefon the ball. It worked. On the year, Stefon tallied 36 catches for 770 yards and 8 receiving touchdowns. He added 277 yards rushing on 17 carries and 3 rushing touchdowns. He also scored a touchdown on a kickoff return and another on a punt return.

He was named to Maryland's All-State first team. *The Washington Post* named him to the All-Metro first team. He was also an All-County selection by the *Montgomery Gazette* community newspaper.

Stefon was more than an offensive wonder. He was awarded the All-Metro Defensive Player of the Year by *The Washington Post*. As a cornerback, he posted 31.5 tackles. He intercepted 4 passes, and he forced 3 fumbles.

The senior's status spread far beyond Maryland and Washington, D.C. Nationwide, Stefon was considered the second-best wide receiver by Scout.com. ESPN ranked him as the third-best athlete in the 2012 class. Rivals.com named him the top recruit in the state of Maryland.

Still, a big question remained: Where would Stefon choose to play football in college?

7

⟨⟨⟨⟨⟨⟨ COLLEGE CHOICE ⟩⟩⟩⟩⟩⟩

The 2012 U.S. Army All-American Bowl was held in San Antonio, Texas, on January 7, 2012. This high school all-star game was nationally televised, and Stefon was proud to be a part of it.

Stefon had been looking forward to this special day for the past year. Donning a black jersey for the East all-stars, Stefon saw action early as a wide receiver and kickoff returner. The game format had players rotating in and out of the lineup often. So Stefon didn't play as much as he typically would.

Midway through the first quarter, Stefon took a handoff on a trick play and exploded around the right end for 21 yards. There was some debate about whether he fumbled at the end of his run, but his team kept the ball. A few plays later, the East squad scored a touchdown.

East kept the game close through much of the first half. But the West team scored 10 points in the final 2 minutes to take a commanding 24–6 lead.

In the second half, West slowed their offense down to minimize East's chances. Penalties and turnovers added to East's troubles. Stefon's squad managed another touchdown late in the game, but they fell to the West team, 24–12.

Throughout the game, several East and West players announced their college choices. Yet Stefon was silent. He remained one of the few who hadn't made his decision.

It wasn't for lack of opportunities. Colleges loaded his mailbox with invitations and scholarship offers. Florida wanted him. The University of Southern California wanted him. Auburn and Ohio State wanted him. His mother kept all of the letters and filled a few large totes with the many offers.

Mrs. Diggs advised Stefon to attend a nearby college. She suggested the University of Maryland. Of course, she wanted to keep her son close. But her reasons were greater than that. She liked Maryland head coach Randy Edsall and offensive coordinator Mike Lockley. Their coaching styles reminded her of Stefon's father.

EXTRA POINT

East wide receivers coach T.J. Lane called Stefon a joy to coach and said that he was East's heart and soul.

She didn't need to worry. Stefon made his decision with his family—and his hometown—in mind. He was like a father to his brothers, and he wanted to stay close to his mother. But there was more than that. Stefon was fiercely loyal to the Maryland fans who supported him.

He told Scout.com, "Where else is a better place to do it than your city . . . your city's always behind you, so it's only right to give back . . . I have the most supporters here, and I feel like I'm gonna do it here . . . you gotta give respect to your hometown [college]."

On February 10, 2012, Stefon signed an agreement called a "letter of intent" to play football for the University of Maryland, College Park. It was a stunning move, and it shocked people across the country.

Stefon could play anywhere he chose. He could play for a team that might win a national championship. Many critics wondered why a player of his talents would pick the Maryland Terrapins, a team whose record was just 2–10 the year before.

Stefon chose to attend the University of Maryland in College Park.

He was also criticized for waiting so long to choose his college—a month or more later than most elite athletes. Some people called him a "diva," a difficult person who was hard to please. Some thought that he was trying to get extra attention.

Most of his critics, though, were college football fans from coast to coast. They were upset that Stefon chose not to play for their favorite teams.

8

⟨⟨⟨⟨⟨ FRESHMAN STANDOUT ⟩⟩⟩⟩⟩

Stefon graduated from high school in May of 2012. A few weeks later, he moved to College Park, Maryland, to begin football practice.

He entered his freshman season as one of Maryland's top recruits of the year—or any year. But while he was a star in his hometown, he remained unproven at the college level. Would he live up to the hype? It would not take long for Stefon to answer.

On September 1, he took the field at Byrd Stadium in College Park for his first college game. The Terrapins' opponent was the William & Mary Tribe from Virginia. While not a stellar game, the Terrapins eked out a 7–6 win. Stefon caught his first pass, for 5 yards, in the first quarter. In all, he contributed 3 yards rushing, 30 yards receiving, and 50 yards in punt returns.

His biggest contribution came in the fourth quarter. His 16-yard reception from quarterback Perry Hills gave the team a first down near the 50-yard line. The play helped to set up the Terrapins' only touchdown of the day, eight plays later.

Week 2 brought them another victory, 36–27, in a road battle against the Temple Owls. Stefon did his part.

He rushed for 17 yards, caught 3 passes for 59 yards, and added another 59 yards in kickoff and punt returns.

His role continued to grow the next week, at home against the Connecticut Huskies. Stefon posted 57 yards receiving, but he truly made his mark on special teams. He returned 3 kickoffs for 98 yards and added 68 yards on 5 punt returns. His play helped to set up excellent field position for the Terrapins all day long. Nevertheless, the team suffered its first loss of the season, 24–21.

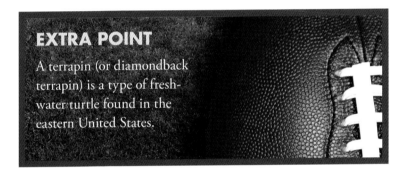

EXTRA POINT

A terrapin (or diamondback terrapin) is a type of freshwater turtle found in the eastern United States.

Maryland dropped its second straight contest a week later, falling to the West Virginia Mountaineers, 31–21. A defeat against the country's 8th-ranked team came as no surprise, but Stefon caught the nation's attention.

The freshman hauled in 3 passes and scored his first two college touchdowns: a 42-yarder and a 56-yard score. Altogether, Stefon went off for 113 yards receiving, 63 yards on kickoff returns, and 25 yards on punt returns. He received the Atlantic Coast Conference (ACC) Rookie of the Week honor, despite the loss.

Stefon's high school coach Bob Milloy attended a game with hopes of talking with his former player. Milloy found a line of at least 150 people waiting to get Stefon's autograph. The young receiver had already elevated to a new level of play in his short time with the Terrapins.

Stefon earned a promotion to starting wide receiver on October 6. He rewarded his coaches with another superb game. The Wake Forest Demon Deacons jumped to an early 7–0 lead. Maryland stormed back with two field goals and a touchdown, giving them a 13–7 edge at halftime.

Midway through the third quarter, Wake Forest added their second touchdown of the day, on a 7-yard pass. A successful extra point gave the Demon Deacons a 1-point lead—and that's where the score remained for a full quarter of play.

The back-and-forth defensive struggle finally turned the Terrapins' way with 7:29 to go in the fourth. On 2nd and 18, Stefon caught a short pass from Hills and burst through the Wake Forest defense. He sprinted his way to the 3-yard line before he was finally stopped. The thrilling 63-yard play set up a touchdown plunge by Justus Pickett. It gave Maryland a 19–14 lead and, eventually, the win.

Stefon finished with 5 catches for 105 yards. For the second straight week, he received ACC Rookie of the Week honors.

The team rode their win into Virginia the next week, and they took that game, 27–20. Stefon managed 3 yards rushing and 89 yards receiving. He also posted 147 yards on 3 kickoff returns, including a 100-yard touchdown return to begin the game. He did not receive Rookie of the Week this time. Instead, he was named ACC Specialist of the Week.

With Maryland's surprising 4–2 start, defenses were quickly learning that Stefon could explode for a big play at any moment. They had to account for the freshman if they hoped to win.

9

⟨⟨⟨⟨⟨ QUARTERBACK ISSUES ⟩⟩⟩⟩⟩

Stefon's mom was right about coaches Edsall and Lockley. They were not content with her son's play. Edsall and Lockley expected him to get better. A complete wide receiver did more than just catch passes and speed past opponents. Stefon needed to block, occupy defenders to help his teammates get open, and stay focused on his role. Edsall and Lockley pushed all of these areas to help Stefon improve every week.

Unfortunately, the road ahead would be challenging, as Maryland's luck was about to change for the worse. While Stefon continued to dominate on the field, injuries plagued the Terrapins in the second half of the season.

Despite Stefon's 149 all-purpose yards, the team lost a heartbreaker to North Carolina State, 20–18. It was a costly loss, as starting quarterback Perry Hills and backup quarterback Devin Burns were both injured, ending their seasons.

Maryland battled Boston College a week later. In the fourth quarter, yet another quarterback was injured. This time, it was freshman Caleb Rowe.

Stefon led all receivers with 152 receiving yards and a touchdown. He also posted 40 yards on kickoff and punt returns. But the Terrapins fell, 20–17. Stefon did, however, receive his third ACC Rookie of the Week honor.

Shawn Petty took the field as quarterback the following week, when Georgia Tech came to town. Petty was a freshman linebacker who had seen action as a quarterback in high school. Petty threw 1 interception and 2 touchdowns, both to Stefon. They were Maryland's only points in a 33–13 loss.

EXTRA POINT

Maryland actually lost its first quarterback, C.J. Brown, to a knee injury before the start of the season.

Along with his 2 touchdowns, Stefon put up 220 all-purpose yards, including 133 on kickoff returns. He did it with an injured ankle, which he suffered early in the game. That didn't stop him from leaping over a defensive back to score his second touchdown.

Stefon's injury kept him out of the 45–10 loss against the Clemson Tigers. But he returned for the game against the Florida State Seminoles. There was some question as to why he would play—and risk compounding the injury—when the season had already become a disaster.

The answer may have been found in Stefon's character. He wanted to be on the field. He wanted to help his teammates. And, of course, he learned from his dad that, if you got knocked down, you didn't cry.

You got up.

You went again.

Stefon finished his freshman season with a 45–38 loss to the North Carolina Tar Heels, but he did so in style. He carried the ball 3 times for 20 yards, caught 8 passes for 82 yards, and returned 4 kickoffs for 146 yards, including a 99-yard touchdown. He also threw an 8-yard pass into the arms of tight end Matt Furstenburg for a touchdown. Stefon ended the day with 256 all-purpose yards, keeping Maryland close in what was supposed to be a Tar Heels blowout.

Playing in 11 of 12 games, with 4 different quarterbacks, Stefon led the Terrapins with 54 receptions, 848 receiving yards, and 6 touchdown receptions (along with 2 touchdowns on kickoff returns). His 1,896 total yards was the second most in Terrapin history.

With an average of 77.1 receiving yards per game, Stefon was fifth best in the ACC. He finished second in the conference and eighth in the country with an average of 172.4 all-purpose yards per game. He was also second in the ACC in kickoff return average at 28.5 yards and fifth in punt returns with a 10-yard average.

All told, it was a successful season for Stefon—but not the season that he would have liked. The team finished with a record of 4–8, but Stefon wanted them to become a winning team. He wanted the nation to look at the Maryland Terrapins as a quality football program, as a contender in the ACC.

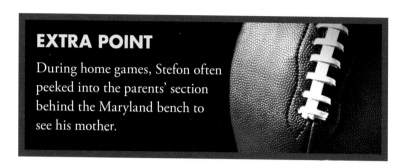

EXTRA POINT

During home games, Stefon often peeked into the parents' section behind the Maryland bench to see his mother.

10

WINNING STREAK

Despite Stefon's achievements on the field, criticism surfaced again among fans and the media. If he had chosen a college with a stable quarterback, if he had gone to a team with more talent, he could have increased his productivity and his own national rankings. He could have played for a winner.

Stefon dwelled on none of that. He was proud to play in his home state, for his home team. During the off-season, he turned his attention to making the Terrapins better. C.J. Brown would be back as starting quarterback. Stefon looked forward to it. He also knew that gaining a rhythm with his quarterback was vital to a successful year.

When he wasn't working out with his brother Trevon, Stefon worked out with Brown. Even before the football season began, Stefon and Brown practiced regularly together. Nearly every day that summer, the two worked on something, both on and off the field.

In an August 2013 article in the *Baltimore Sun*, Stefon said that his time with Brown would make a big difference in the season ahead. The quarterback would know how Stefon ran his routes and would know exactly where to throw the football.

On August 31, Stefon and the Terrapins hosted the Florida International University Panthers in their first game of the new season. The Terrapins dominated from beginning to end. In the 43–10 win, Stefon led both teams with 194 all-purpose yards, including 98 receiving yards, 70 on kickoff returns, and a single rush for 26 yards.

Week 2 found the Terrapins at home once again. And once again they blew out the competition, crushing Old Dominion, 47–10. Stefon led all receivers with 6 catches for 179 yards, including a 41-yard touchdown. He was honored as the ACC Receiver of the Week.

This season wasn't just about Stefon. It was about the team, about the wins. This was about Stefon's goal to make the Terrapins a force in the conference.

Week 3 against Connecticut wasn't quite a blowout, but the Terrapins extended their winning record to 3–0 with a 32–21 victory. Stefon scored his third touchdown in three games with a 12-yard catch in the third quarter. In total, Stefon tallied 145 all-purpose yards: 110 receiving and 35 on kickoff returns.

The Terrapins played a home game in Baltimore in Week 4. Their opponent was West Virginia, a team that had beaten them seven games in a row. This year, however, was different. Maryland trounced the Mountaineers, 37–0. Stefon had a quiet game, posting only 17 total yards.

A day later, Coach Edsall announced that Stefon had suffered a minor injury. Fans and commentators couldn't help but wonder if it was more serious than the coach was letting on. After all, Stefon wasn't being utilized as much as before. For example, he didn't seem to be the primary punt returner anymore.

Still, the team was 4–0. It was very likely that they would qualify for a post-season bowl game—a special event that teams with six or more wins were invited to participate in. This was another goal that Stefon held for the team.

Stefon prepares to take a handoff on a trick play.

INJURIES

Maryland next traveled to play against Florida State. It was another blowout—this time in the wrong direction. The 8th-ranked Seminoles steamrolled the Terrapins, 63–0. Stefon was held to 29 all-purpose yards.

This was a crushing defeat for Stefon's team. Florida State exposed Maryland's weaknesses and left the players feeling deflated. To make matters worse, quarterback C.J. Brown was injured in the second quarter. He stayed out the remainder of the game and did not play in their next matchup, against Virginia.

Even without him, Maryland improved to 5–1 in Week 6, edging Virginia by a score of 27–26. It was not a pretty win, but it still counted. Stefon again did not play in top form, but he managed 96 receiving yards and 158 all-purpose yards.

Week 7 found the Terrapins in North Carolina, taking on the Wake Forest Demon Deacons. Maryland fell behind, 10–0, in the first quarter. But they started the second quarter strong, quickly gaining two first downs and moving into Wake Forest territory.

With the Terrapins driving toward a score, Brandon Ross carried the ball for a 9-yard gain. But tragedy struck on the play. Wide receiver Deon Long went down with a broken leg. Stefon rushed to his friend's side. He leaned over and offered words of encouragement before his teammate was driven off the field on a cart.

After play resumed, Maryland drove to the 4-yard line but were unable to reach the end zone. They kicked a field goal, cutting the lead to 10–3.

Later in the quarter, 2 interceptions by quarterback C.J. Brown led to 2 touchdowns for Wake Forest. The home team led, 24–3, heading into the second half.

C.J. Brown was replaced by Caleb Rowe in the third quarter. Rowe threw a 56-yard touchdown, but Wake Forest answered immediately and methodically. They took nearly 5 minutes off the clock as they traveled 88 yards for another touchdown. The quarter ended with the Demon Deacons on top, 31–10.

By then, Stefon had posted 178 yards: 67 receiving and 111 on kickoff returns. Early in the fourth quarter, Stefon pushed a defender out of his way as he ran a short crossing route. Rowe zipped the football to him, and Stefon made the catch. He turned to run and was pulled down from behind . . .

Pop!

Stefon felt the sound in his right leg as much as he heard it. He stayed on the ground.

Two hours after Deon Long broke his leg, Stefon broke his fibula too. Long's season was over, and so was Stefon's. The Terrapins had lost their two leading receivers.

Maryland fell, 34–10. Hopes for a bowl game were suddenly much bleaker.

The Terrapins lost three of their final five games and ended the regular season with a record of 7–5. It was a vast improvement over the previous year, but injuries left the team wondering how good they could have been.

They were invited to participate in the Military Bowl on December 27. Stefon's goal for the team had been accomplished. It was unfortunate that he could not play in the game. Without him, the Terrapins lost to the Marshall Thundering Herd, 31–20.

Although he missed nearly half the season, Stefon's exceptional play was recognized both by coaches and the media. He was an "honorable mention" selection to the All-ACC team.

EXTRA POINT

In 2013, Stefon's brother Trevon told the *Baltimore Sun* that the one player he most wanted to be was his brother.

12

ROAD TO RECOVERY

It would be easy for Stefon to give up after an injury like that. He went to class on crutches or even riding in a vehicle similar to a golf cart. The pain kept him awake at night. He couldn't take a shower without help. He was tired. He was dejected. But he kept going.

Over time, Stefon began to see the injury as more of a blessing. It allowed him to slow down and take a deep look at himself. During the season, Stefon's schedule was filled with classes, practices, meetings, and games. Now, he was able to consider the most important people in his life, to think about who were his best friends. He gained a new appreciation for them—and for the sport he desperately longed to play.

Coach Edsall mirrored Stefon's thoughts in a *USA Today* article. Edsall said that Stefon appreciated everything a little more. Edsall saw a mature young man, who realized that he wasn't invincible and that the game could be taken away in an instant.

Stefon and Long spent a lot of time together. They watched home football games at the stadium, and they watched away games, cheering at a TV screen. They raced each other to class on crutches and went to treatments

Testudo is the official mascot of the University of Maryland.

together. They were close friends, and they kept each other motivated while they rehabilitated their legs.

Long expressed how important that was to him in the same *USA Today* article. "You do feel kind of isolated," Long said. "Having your best friend right there with you makes it so much better."

After 3 months of grueling rehab, Stefon accomplished something that had been impossible for so long: he put on his own shoes.

During Stefon's recovery, Edsall and Lockley continued to work with him. They had him practice with the second team offense. It gave Stefon time to heal. It also helped the up-and-coming players to learn from Stefon and improve their skills too.

By the end of spring practice, both Stefon and Long were well enough to play. Stefon used the summer months to work with Long daily. Together, they regained their speed, strength, and confidence.

By the time his junior season began, Stefon felt even faster than before he was injured.

Stefon became the "face" of Maryland football—the featured athlete. In a year that the Terrapins moved from the ACC to the Big Ten Conference, Stefon's image appeared on the team's marketing and merchandise. His jersey was sold in three different colors. In August, during Fan Appreciation Day, the line for Stefon's autograph stretched across the field.

Stefon was also the focal point of a "Stay at Home" movement. The campaign encouraged Maryland's talented high school athletes to play for the Terrapins and help to build up the program, rather than go to high-profile colleges in other states. The movement, which Stefon was often credited with starting, came to national attention in July 2014. Stefon tweeted in support of basketball superstar (and Ohio native) Lebron James' return to the Cleveland Cavaliers, and the country took notice.

Stefon said that he could relate to James, a player who chose his new team in the interest of family and friends—not just what was best for him. The sentiment reflected upon Stefon's own decision to play for Maryland, soundly quieting those who had criticized him in the past.

So on that Fan Appreciation Day, Stefon's busy line of autograph seekers had as much to do with his performance off the field as it did on the field. Hometown pride ran deep, and Stefon showed that his ran deeper than most.

On the edge of his junior season, the star receiver was determined to give Maryland even more reason to be proud. Despite injuries and quarterback issues, Stefon was closing in on no less than 20 university records. He had already tied the record for most touchdowns on kickoff returns in a single season (2), and he held the top spot for most yards per kickoff return in his career (26.9). With a full season ahead, he would surely cement his place in the Terrapin record books.

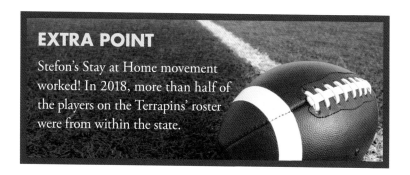

EXTRA POINT

Stefon's Stay at Home movement worked! In 2018, more than half of the players on the Terrapins' roster were from within the state.

13

〈〈〈〈〈 BIG TEN 〉〉〉〉〉

Now in a new conference, the Terrapins had an even tougher schedule. The Big Ten was a football powerhouse, so Maryland would face opponents like Iowa, Michigan, Michigan State, Ohio State, and Wisconsin. Stefon and the Terrapins had their work cut out for them.

Their first contest was at home against the James Madison Bulldogs on August 30, 2014. While Stefon led the receivers with 5 catches for 53 yards, Maryland brought a more balanced attack to the field. C.J. Brown rushed for 3 touchdowns, and Deon Long caught a 41-yard touchdown pass. The Terrapins controlled the game, winning 52–7.

Against South Florida the next week, Maryland put another notch in the win column, 24–17. Stefon caught 7 passes for 50 yards and gained 65 more on 2 kickoff returns.

At home in Week 3, Maryland faced their old foes, the West Virginia Mountaineers. Stefon took up his familiar role of leading receiver, this time with 5 catches for 127 yards and a touchdown—a 77-yarder from C.J. Brown. Unfortunately, West Virginia led the entire game, winning a close one, 40–37.

The Terrapins beat Syracuse, 34–20, in Week 4. They then crushed their first Big Ten opponent, Indiana, by a score of 37–15. Stefon scored a touchdown in the second quarter on a 29-yard pass from C.J. Brown. He finished with 112 yards receiving on 6 catches.

That set up a contest on October 4 between the 4–1 Terrapins and the 3–1 Ohio State University (OSU) Buckeyes. OSU coach Urban Meyer had heavily recruited Stefon in high school and thought that he had a good chance at signing him. But all the incentives and promises were not enough to overcome Stefon's desire to stay home.

EXTRA POINT

Some 2 years later, OSU still seemed to sting from Stefon's decision. Prior to the game, several media outlets spoke about what might have been.

Stefon's decision didn't hurt the Buckeyes. The team won 24 straight games in 2012 and 2013. But they still hadn't found a wide receiver as talented as Stefon.

Before the game, Meyer had only positive things to say about Stefon. He said that Stefon was as "good as there is in America." Meyer also predicted that Stefon could be a first-round pick whenever he entered the NFL draft.

From the Maryland star's perspective, it was just another game. He was excited to play against such a good opponent. But questions about how weird it would be to play against a coach who so heavily pursued him fell flat. Stefon didn't think it was weird at all. In fact, he seemed to have as much respect for Meyer as Meyer had for him. Still, he planned to do his best to show them what they missed out on.

Unfortunately for Stefon and the Terrapins, things didn't go as planned.

The Buckeyes held Stefon to 90 total yards: 38 yards on kickoff returns and 52 yards receiving on 7 receptions. One of his catches went for a 4-yard touchdown in the fourth quarter, but it was too little, too late.

Maryland threw 4 interceptions, and OSU controlled the football for much of the day. The Terrapins fell, 52–24, in a game that was never in doubt.

It was not the outcome that Stefon's squad was looking for, but it was just one game. They were still 4–2 when the Iowa Hawkeyes came to town.

The game against the Hawkeyes did not start well. On the first play from scrimmage, C.J. Brown threw an interception that set up a 4-yard touchdown run for Iowa. Midway through the quarter, Iowa scored again, giving them a 14–0 lead.

Maryland needed to do something they had not done all season: overcome a double-digit deficit—and opponent momentum—to get back into the game.

The Terrapins scored a rushing touchdown before the end of the first quarter, then added a field goal early in the second. Four minutes later, the Terrapins put another touchdown on the board, giving them a 17–14 lead. They never looked back.

Maryland was ultimately victorious, 38–31. Stefon caught 9 passes for 130 yards, including a 53-yard touchdown reception in the third quarter. He also returned a kickoff for 21 yards.

Stefon dodges defenders on his way to a big gain.

It was an impressive win against a quality opponent, but the team's confidence and momentum didn't carry into the next week. The Wisconsin Badgers decimated the Terrapins, 52–7.

Maryland's only score came with less than a minute to go in the fourth quarter. Stefon caught a 21-yard pass from C.J. Brown. It was Stefon's only catch of the day, although he did return 5 kickoffs for 138 yards and rushed twice for 4 yards in the defeat.

The loss dropped Stefon's team to 5–3, and the season suddenly felt like it was headed in the wrong direction. Something had to change. And it did against Penn State University—but not for the better.

14

⟨⟨⟨⟨⟨⟨ SHAKEGATE ⟩⟩⟩⟩⟩⟩

Tempers were hot against the Penn State Nittany Lions before the game even began. The two teams got into a brief scuffle coming onto the field.

A short while later, Penn State's team captains met Maryland's captains—including Stefon—in the middle of the field. The Nittany Lions players held out their hands, expecting a handshake. Stefon and his two co-captains simply stared at them.

Penn State dropped their hands, and the referees threw a flag. Maryland was penalized 15 yards for unsportsmanlike conduct, and the game hadn't even begun.

The Nittany Lions started strong, marching 36 yards for a field goal. They added two more field goals in the first half, while Maryland managed a touchdown. At halftime, Penn State led, 9–7.

The game teetered back and forth in the second half. Penn State scored a touchdown in the third quarter, extending their lead.

Maryland came back in the fourth with a field goal and a touchdown, taking the lead, 17–16. But they were unable to keep Penn State from putting another field goal on the board with 6 minutes left to play.

To make matters worse, Stefon injured his kidney. He was in extreme pain after getting hit while stretching for the end zone.

With the game on the line, the Terrapins coolly drove into Penn State territory and advanced the football into scoring position. In the game's final minute, kicker Brad Craddock knocked a 43-yard field goal through the uprights. It gave Maryland the lead and the win, 20–19.

The team celebrated at midfield, where the captains had refused to shake hands with their opponents. The Terrapins were 6–3, and the win qualified the team for a post-season bowl game.

EXTRA POINT

When Maryland's captains refused to shake hands at the beginning of the game, it became known as "ShakeGate" across the country. Coach Edsall and Stefon later apologized for their actions. The university was fined $10,000 for the unsportsmanlike display.

Stefon posted 75 yards on 4 kickoff returns, and he caught 6 passes for 53 yards. These would be the last regular-season yards that Stefon would accumulate. He was suspended for the team's next game, against Michigan State, because of the pregame scuffle. But Stefon would not have played anyway. His injury sidelined him for the rest of the regular season.

The Terrapins finished their schedule with a respectable record of 7–5. They were invited to participate in the Foster Farms Bowl against Stanford on December 30.

With nearly 2 months to recover from his injury, Stefon was able to suit up and play. He made a difference too, catching 10 passes for 138 yards. But the talented Stanford team was too much for Maryland. The Cardinals scored three unanswered touchdowns in the second quarter, and the Terrapins never recovered. They lost, 45–21.

In 2014, Stefon again paced Maryland's receiving unit with 52 receptions for 654 yards and 5 touchdowns. He was selected to the All-Big Ten second team.

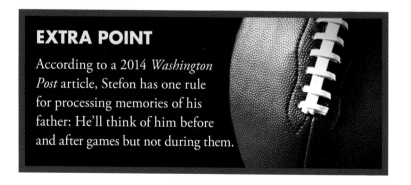

EXTRA POINT

According to a 2014 *Washington Post* article, Stefon has one rule for processing memories of his father: He'll think of him before and after games but not during them.

15

⟨⟨⟨⟨⟨ COLLEGE OR PRO ⟩⟩⟩⟩⟩

With his junior season behind him, Stefon faced a difficult choice. He still had one more year of college football left. But he was now eligible to play in the National Football League (NFL).

If he stayed in college, he risked getting injured again. A severe injury could keep him from ever playing in the NFL. But if he chose professional football, he couldn't change his mind and return to Maryland. His college career would be over.

By choosing professional football, Stefon would enter the NFL draft. For seven rounds, each NFL team would have an opportunity to pick a former college player for their roster. Stefon had enough talent for the league, but would his college injuries prevent teams from drafting him? And because of the Penn State incident, there were questions about his character and attitude too.

The National Collegiate Athletic Association (NCAA) determined that football athletes had approximately a 1.6 percent chance of being drafted.

Despite the unfavorable odds, Stefon chose to skip his senior season at Maryland. He declared himself eligible for the NFL draft. He knew he wouldn't be a first-round choice. But he certainly believed that he would get picked in the second round—or maybe the third round—of the draft. After all, Stefon finished his career with 150 catches for 2,227 yards and 14 receiving touchdowns. Those numbers ranked in Maryland's top five of all-time. Stefon also finished fourth in career kickoff return yardage, with 1,472 yards.

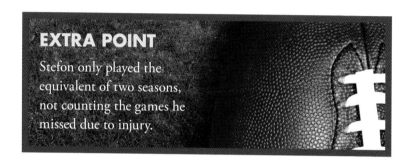

EXTRA POINT

Stefon only played the equivalent of two seasons, not counting the games he missed due to injury.

The 2015 NFL draft began with Round 1 on April 30. Rounds 2 and 3 were held a day later. Stefon's family was confident that his name would be called on Day 2, so they threw him a party at home. They gathered in front of the television and excitedly watched.

One receiver after another was chosen: Devin Smith to the Jets. Dorial Green-Beckham to Tennessee. Devin Funchess to Carolina. Eight wide receivers were chosen in Rounds 2 and 3. Stefon's name was never called.

The party fizzled out. The rooms were cleaned. Food was put away. The television, mercifully, was turned off.

On the third day of the draft, Stefon decided not to sit around and wait. No amount of tears, he remembered, would change the situation. He decided to go out and exercise. He tried to get his mind off the previous day's disappointment.

Round 4 came and went. Then Round 5 began. Ten picks in, the Minnesota Vikings made one of the best picks of the entire weekend: Stefon Diggs. He was the 19th receiver selected and the 146th player overall.

Maryland fans were disappointed. Sure, they wanted to see Stefon in purple—Baltimore Ravens' purple. But instead of drafting Stefon, the Ravens opted for Breshad Perriman, a wide receiver from Central Florida.

Stefon's family also would have enjoyed seeing Stefon play in his home state. According to *Sports Illustrated*, Mrs. Diggs later met Ravens general manager Ozzie Newsome, the person in charge of Baltimore's draft selections. She boldly told him, "You didn't pick my son. They should fire [you]!"

The Vikings signed Stefon to a 4-year contract worth $2.5 million. They hoped that he could make a difference as a rookie, a first-year player in the league.

16

⟨⟨⟨⟨⟨ LOOKING GOOD ⟩⟩⟩⟩⟩

After a variety of practices throughout May, June, and July, the Vikings' preseason schedule began in August 2015. The five preseason games were essentially practice contests that didn't really count as wins or losses.

In a 14–3 game over Pittsburgh, Stefon caught 2 passes for 14 yards and returned 2 punts for 66 yards.

Game 2 had Minnesota playing at TCF Bank Stadium in Minneapolis. It served as the team's temporary home field while the new U.S. Bank Stadium was being built. Stefon caught 2 passes for 26 yards. He tacked on another 55 yards on 2 punt returns, the longest of which was 37 yards. The result was a 26–16 victory over the Tampa Bay Buccaneers.

Stefon made a solid impression on the road against the Dallas Cowboys. He caught 3 passes for 49 yards, returned a kickoff for 22 yards, and ran back 3 punts for 38 yards. Minnesota won the game, 28–14.

His best performance of the preseason came against the Tennessee Titans. Stefon was an offensive standout, leading the team with 8 receptions for 85 yards. He scored a touchdown on a 7-yard pass from reserve quarterback Taylor Heinicke, but the Vikings fell, 24–17.

Despite shining in the preseason, Stefon did not play in Minnesota's first three games of the regular season. Five wide receivers were ahead of him on the depth chart, so there wasn't room for Stefon. The Vikings went 2–1 in those games.

Coming into Week 4, a hip injury to wide receiver Charles Johnson created a spot in the lineup for Stefon. The former Terrapin made his NFL debut in Denver on October 4, against the Broncos—one of the league's best teams. Stefon took full advantage of the opportunity.

With 6:22 to go in the first quarter, he caught a short pass from quarterback Teddy Bridgewater. The play only went for 2 yards, but it was Stefon's first official reception in the NFL.

The Broncos ground their way to a 13–0 lead in the second quarter. But in the final minutes of the first half, Bridgewater connected with Stefon deep down the middle of the field. The 25-yard gain set up a Vikings field goal.

A few plays later, an interception led to the Vikings' first touchdown. As the second quarter came to an end, the Broncos held onto the lead, 13–10.

Denver opened the third quarter with a 62-yard drive that resulted in another touchdown. Minnesota rallied in the fourth quarter with 10 points to tie the game, 20–20. But the Broncos kicked a field goal with less than 2 minutes on the clock. The Vikings fell, 23–20.

Despite the loss, Stefon played very well against a stout defense. He caught 6 passes for 87 yards and led the

Vikings in total yards from scrimmage. For a team that featured All-Pro running back Adrian Peterson, that was an impressive feat.

Stefon played even better the following week. Against the Kansas City Chiefs, he caught 7 passes for 129 yards. His performance helped Minnesota to a 16–10 victory.

Next, the Vikings traveled to Detroit. Early in the third quarter, the Vikings trailed, 17–15. With the ball on the Lions' 36-yard line, Bridgewater dropped back to pass. He spotted Stefon streaking down the left sideline and heaved a pass in his direction. The pass was thrown too hard, just out of Stefon's reach. But Stefon leaped, stretched as far as he could, and snagged the ball with his fingertips. He hauled it in and secured it tightly before landing in the end zone. It was Stefon's first NFL touchdown—and what a catch it was.

Minnesota defeated Detroit, 28–19. Stefon contributed 108 receiving yards on 6 receptions.

EXTRA POINT

Stefon loves to compete. He even turns regular, everyday activities into contests. He has raced his family and friends in everything from tying shoes to drinking water.

With a record of 4–2, the Vikings visited Chicago to battle the Bears. Stefon's sudden emergence allowed his team to become more balanced on offense. In the past, the Vikings had to rely mostly on the running of Peterson. Stefon's exceptional play allowed the Vikings to distribute the football more evenly around the field.

Chicago led 20–13 with 2 minutes to go in the game. From the Bears' 40-yard line, Bridgewater dropped back to pass. He zipped the ball 10 yards downfield to Stefon. The speedy receiver juked right to avoid a tackler. The field opened up in front of him, and he raced forward. He bulled his way through a couple of defenders near the goal line and crossed into the end zone.

Touchdown!

The Vikings defense forced the Bears to punt after just three plays. Then as the final seconds ticked off the clock, the offense covered 48 yards in 4 plays. Blair Walsh kicked the game-winning field goal as time expired.

With Chicago's defense unable to key on Peterson, the running back gained 103 yards on the ground. Stefon chipped in with 95 yards receiving in the 23–20 win.

EXTRA POINT

Stefon loves Starbucks coffee shops. He sometimes jokes that he and Starbucks are both "open all day."

17

⟨⟨⟨⟨⟨ PLAYOFF PUSH ⟩⟩⟩⟩⟩

In his first four games, Stefon led the Vikings with 419 yards receiving. He became the first wide receiver in NFL history to gain at least 85 yards receiving in each of his first four games. Even though he did not play in the first three games, he ranked second among all rookies in receiving yards. He was already being compared to a sensational rookie from the previous season: Odell Beckham, Jr.

Stefon's first "quiet" game came against the Rams. He was held to 3 receptions for 42 yards. Yet the Vikings won in an overtime thriller, 21–18.

Halfway through the season, Stefon and his team were 6–2. They were tied with Minnesota's arch rival, the Green Bay Packers, for first place in the North division of the National Football Conference (NFC).

The Vikings took their next game, too, defeating the Oakland Raiders, 30–14, behind the power of Adrian Peterson's rushing and Blair Walsh's kicking. Stefon ran the ball once for 10 yards and had 2 receptions for 46.

The script was flipped against the Green Bay Packers. The Vikings were soundly defeated, 30–13. The team's five-game winning streak came to an end, and they fell into second place in the NFC North.

Minnesota bounced back with a victory against the Atlanta Falcons. But they followed that with their worst performance of the season. They were demolished at home against the Seattle Seahawks, 38–7.

The skid continued versus the Arizona Cardinals. The ice-cold Vikings dropped a heartbreaker, 23–20.

Minnesota was 8–5 and trending downward. The once promising season was suddenly in doubt. The team needed to make a change—and they needed to make it quickly.

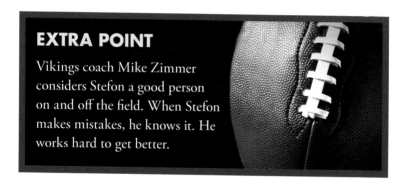

EXTRA POINT

Vikings coach Mike Zimmer considers Stefon a good person on and off the field. When Stefon makes mistakes, he knows it. He works hard to get better.

At home against the Chicago Bears, Stefon caught 3 passes for 55 yards. One of those catches went for a 15-yard touchdown in the first quarter. Another was a short catch and run that went for a 33-yard score. The Vikings won handily, 38–17.

The team rode that win into the next week, taking on the New York Giants at TCF Bank Stadium. Minnesota dominated the visiting team, 49–17. The team's record now stood at 10–5.

They were on a roll and were assured of a playoff berth. Yet the Packers still remained tied with the Vikings in the standings. The two teams squared off in Green Bay for their final game of the regular season. The teams were playing for the NFC North championship and a chance to host a home playoff game.

The hard-fought contest was a defensive struggle from the start. Minnesota held a slim edge at halftime, 6–3. It seemed only fitting that the key play of the game was made by a pair of defensive standouts. In the third quarter, Vikings defensive end Everson Griffen sacked Green Bay quarterback Aaron Rodgers, causing a fumble. The ball floated forward and looked to most players and fans like an incomplete pass. But Vikings cornerback Captain Munnerlyn smartly scooped up the loose ball and returned it 55 yards for a touchdown. It was one of two Minnesota touchdowns in the third quarter.

Minnesota held off a late Green Bay rally. They won the game—and the division—by a score of 20–13.

The playoffs began the following week, and Minnesota hosted the Seattle Seahawks. The infamous game, played in the bitter January cold, was dominated by the Vikings in every way except the scoreboard.

Minnesota built a 9–0 lead over three quarters. But costly mistakes allowed Seattle to rally for 10 points in the fourth. Nevertheless, the Vikings were in position to win in the closing seconds of the game. However, the season ended when the kicker missed a short 27-yard field goal.

For the year, Stefon had 52 receptions for 720 yards and scored 4 touchdowns. He gained 13 yards rushing on 3 attempts and 22 yards on a kickoff return—a total of 755 all-purpose yards. He was named to the Pro Football Writers of America All-Rookie Team.

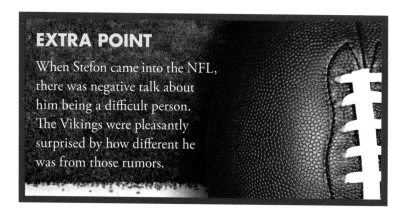

EXTRA POINT

When Stefon came into the NFL, there was negative talk about him being a difficult person. The Vikings were pleasantly surprised by how different he was from those rumors.

18

⟨⟨⟨⟨⟨ YEAR TWO ⟩⟩⟩⟩⟩

The 2016 season was not the breakout year Vikings fans hoped it would be. Remaining healthy proved to be a challenge for the team.

The flurry of injuries began before the first snap of the season. On August 30, Teddy Bridgewater severely injured his knee during a practice. He had been considered the quarterback who could guide the Vikings back to the playoffs. Now he was out for the season.

Minnesota went into emergency mode and traded for quarterback Sam Bradford from the Philadelphia Eagles. The trade came just 10 days before Minnesota's first game.

Stefon keyed the offense in the Week 1 matchup versus the Tennessee Titans. He hauled in 7 catches for 103 yards. The Vikings won, 25–16.

Stefon elevated his play the next week for the first ever game in Minnesota's new home, U.S. Bank Stadium. Fittingly enough, the opponent was Green Bay.

Stefon sliced through the Packers defense for 182 yards on 9 receptions, including a 25-yard touchdown catch. Behind Bradford's stellar play, the Vikings won, 17–14.

The win was not without a price, however. In the third quarter, running back Adrian Peterson tore his lateral meniscus—a band of cartilage on the outside of the knee. Like Bridgewater, Peterson's season came to an early end. With nine players already on injured reserve, losing their star rusher was a crushing blow.

Even without their key offensive weapon, Minnesota went on to win the next three games. They earned their fifth victory of the season, against the Houston Texans, without Stefon. He was sidelined with an injury to his thigh muscles.

For Stefon, the bye week came at the perfect time. He had an opportunity to rest and recover his body. Yet more importantly, his life changed forever. On October 14, Stefon began a family of his own. His first child was born: a daughter.

Meanwhile, the Vikings were 5–0. They were the last unbeaten team in the league. But how long could they keep winning with so many players injured?

The answer came abruptly.

U.S. Bank Stadium

Despite Stefon's return to the starting lineup, the team dropped four games in a row. The receiver posted 8 catches for 76 yards against the Bears. He added 13 receptions for 80 yards versus Detroit. Neither performance could snap the losing skid.

Due to the earlier injury, Stefon was not at full speed for the rest of the year. Unable to separate from defenders, he was no longer a threat to go deep down the field. Yet he remained one of the most productive members of the team. Against the Washington Redskins, he caught 13 passes for 164 yards. Still, the Vikings were defeated, 26–20.

The team finally snapped the losing streak against the Arizona Cardinals, winning 30–24. But Stefon had to sit out the next game due to a knee injury, a Thanksgiving contest against Detroit. The Vikings lost 16–13.

Stefon would miss one more game during the season, as the Vikings dropped three of their final five games. They finished at 8–8 and missed the playoffs.

Even injured, Stefon put up some impressive numbers. He led the Vikings in catches with 84 and tallied 903 yards receiving.

EXTRA POINT

Injuries in 2016 created opportunities for players like wide receiver Adam Thielen. He finished with 967 yards receiving.

19

〰〰 CHAMPIONSHIP RUN 〰〰

Football was all the buzz in Minnesota as the 2017 season began. The NFL's championship game, the Super Bowl, would be held at U.S. Bank Stadium. No one knew what to expect from the Vikings. They had been an average team the year before, and many experts believed that they were about the same this year.

Minnesota hosted the New Orleans Saints for their first game of the regular season. With most of the team healthy, the Vikings put together an impressive 29–19 win. Quarterback Sam Bradford played one of his best games as a pro, and Stefon caught 7 passes for 93 yards, including touchdowns of 18 yards and 2 yards.

Unfortunately, Bradford injured his knee. While he was able to finish the game, he was sidelined for much of the season.

Backup quarterback Case Keenum took the field in Pittsburgh against the Steelers. He had very little time to prepare for the start because Bradford was made inactive just a short while before the game. It made sense, then, that Minnesota went from one of the best offenses in the league to one of the worst. They fell, 26–9, in a dismal performance.

Stefon celebrates a touchdown catch against Washington.

The change in quarterback, and the loss, summoned memories of the previous year, making Vikings fans more than a little nervous.

Week 3 may not have settled those nerves, but Keenum gave fans a glimmer of hope. He connected with Stefon 8 times for 173 yards and 2 touchdowns. The inconsistent offense once again looked unstoppable as Minnesota rolled over Tampa Bay, 34–17, at U.S. Bank Stadium.

But another disappointing performance the following week had Vikings fans scratching their heads. Minnesota fell to Detroit, 14–7. On top of that, rookie running back Dalvin Cook was lost to injury. Fans everywhere groaned. It looked like it was going to be another frustrating season.

Against the Chicago Bears, the Vikings put together yet another shaky performance. The offense struggled, and Stefon tweaked the muscle injury that had troubled him throughout 2016. The only good news was that the team managed to pull out a win, 20–17.

Stefon sat out the next two games: a 23–10 win over Green Bay and a 24–16 victory over Baltimore. He returned in a limited capacity to play versus the Cleveland Browns, catching 4 passes for 27 yards. The Vikings won that game too, 33–16, ending the first half of their season with an excellent 6–2 record.

Of course, Vikings fans had seen strong starts turn into disappointing seasons. But this year, there was no need to worry. Stefon and his talented team were heating up.

The Vikings visited Washington, D.C., on November 12 to play the Redskins. The stadium was 30 miles from where Stefon attended high school, so 17 friends and family members came to cheer him on. Stefon hoped to score a touchdown for them.

He nearly did in the first quarter. Stefon raced down the field and caught a 51-yard bomb from Case Keenum. But the play ended at the 2-yard line. Minnesota scored a touchdown two plays later.

Early in the second quarter, trailing 10–7, Keenum connected with Stefon for a 3-yard touchdown pass. After the score, Stefon swooped like an airplane through the end zone, jumped onto the goal post and hugged it before dropping onto his back. Some thought the celebration was too much. For Stefon, it was an extra special play. He had given his many guests something to remember.

He finished the game with 4 receptions for 78 yards, and the Vikings won, 38–30.

With confidence on their side, Minnesota rolled through the rest of the season, winning six of seven contests. Stefon dodged injury and played in every remaining game.

In Week 17, against Chicago, Stefon caught his 200th pass in his 40th game. It made him the fastest player in Vikings history to reach 200 receptions, surpassing even the great Randy Moss.

The Vikings finished 13–3. They were NFC North champions for the second time in 3 years. Stefon totaled 64 receptions for 849 yards and 8 touchdowns.

Minnesota headed into the postseason, firmly in charge of their own destiny. They had a bye in the first round, and they would play at least one home game. If they won two playoff games, they would become the first team ever to play a Super Bowl in their home stadium.

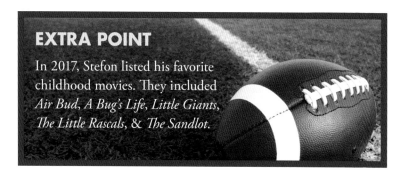

EXTRA POINT

In 2017, Stefon listed his favorite childhood movies. They included *Air Bud*, *A Bug's Life*, *Little Giants*, *The Little Rascals*, & *The Sandlot*.

20

⟨⟨⟨⟨⟨ MIRACLE ⟩⟩⟩⟩⟩

On January 14, 2018, the Vikings took the field at U.S. Bank Stadium for a contest that would become historic. Their opponent was the New Orleans Saints.

Minnesota started with great field position on their own 45-yard line. They took 4 minutes and 15 seconds to march down the field. Running back Jerick McKinnon capped the drive with a 14-yard rushing touchdown.

Stefon caught his first pass in the next series, a 17-yarder that gave the Vikings a first down on their 40. The drive ended with a 20-yard Kai Forbath field goal.

In the second quarter, running back Latavius Murray pushed the ball into the end zone from the 1-yard line. The Vikings led, 17–0.

The score held until halftime, and Minnesota started the second half with the ball. They took nearly 7 minutes to travel to the Saints' 29-yard line. But a penalty and a sack knocked them back to the 40. Rather than risk a long field goal attempt, the Vikings opted to punt.

Saints quarterback Drew Brees led his team into the end zone but took almost the rest of the quarter to do it. With 1:23 on the clock, he connected with wide receiver Michael Thomas for a 14-yard touchdown.

After that, it took one play to turn the game on its ear.

With 1:18 left in the third, Keenum targeted Stefon 17 yards deep. His pass was picked off by Marcus Williams of the Saints, who returned it 12 yards.

A few plays later, early in the fourth quarter, Brees again connected with Thomas for a score. The extra point cut Minnesota's lead to 3 points.

Keenum and the Vikings answered by driving to the Saints 31. Forbath kicked a field goal and added another 3 points to the Vikings' lead.

Later in the quarter, a partially blocked punt set up New Orleans with excellent field position. Brees did not let the opportunity pass. In four plays, he finished the drive with a 14-yard touchdown toss to running back Alvin Kamara. The Saints had their first lead of the day, 21–20, with 3 minutes left.

The Vikings stormed down the field in a minute and a half. Forbath kicked another field goal to put Minnesota back on top, 23–21.

It was up to the defense to hold New Orleans scoreless, and the game would be won.

That didn't happen.

One minute later, the Saints made a 43-yard field goal. With 29 seconds on the clock, the Saints led, 24–23.

The Vikings had one more chance, but it didn't start well. After the kickoff, a penalty pushed Minnesota back to their 20-yard line.

Keenum hit Stefon for 19 yards down the middle of the field. With the clock's final seconds ticking away, the team was forced to use their last timeout.

The clock stopped with 18 seconds left. First and 10 at their own 39-yard line, there was still a long way to go: 61 yards, to be exact.

The football was snapped, and Keenum targeted wide receiver Jarius Wright. Incomplete. Fourteen seconds left.

On the next play, Keenum threw to McKinnon. This too fell incomplete. Ten seconds remained.

The Vikings huddled. Keenum called the play, "Gun Buffalo Right Key Left Seven Heaven." Then he looked at Stefon. "I'm going to give somebody a shot."

Stefon didn't think Keenum would throw to him. The primary target on this play was Adam Thielen.

The football was snapped. Thielen was covered well. Keenum threw deep to Stefon.

The talented receiver made a leaping grab and pulled the ball to his body. The defender behind him missed the tackle. Stefon stumbled, regained his balance, and raced down the field and into the end zone.

Stefon dropped the ball, ripped off his helmet, and stood, soaking in the roar of the crowd. Then he was mobbed by his teammates in celebration.

Somehow, the Vikings had done the impossible. They had won the game, 29–24. As Vikings radio announcer Paul Allen said, it was a miracle. A Minneapolis Miracle.

21

If the play felt unreal to Vikings fans, it was even more so for Stefon, who snagged 6 receptions for 137 yards—and, of course, the touchdown.

Time seemed to slow down after the game. Stefon went out to celebrate with his team and then returned home. He couldn't sleep. He tried to process what had happened and how it happened. He watched the video of the play, again and again.

That was him catching the ball. That was him stumbling. That was him running into the end zone. That was him, no doubt about it. But it felt like he was watching someone else. He remembered each moment, but it seemed as if he was watching a movie.

Sleep finally claimed him somewhere between 4 and 5 in the morning.

It was the first playoff game in NFL history that ended with a game-winning touchdown. The Vikings were also the first team to come within a game of playing in the Super Bowl on their home field.

"Minneapolis Miracle" merchandise popped up for sale throughout the state and across the country.

As thrilling as the play was, it also came with negative consequences. Minnesota still had another game: the NFC championship against the Philadelphia Eagles. Unfortunately, the team didn't perform well. They were flat and perhaps emotionally drained.

They lost to the Eagles, 38–7. The dream season came to an end.

Nevertheless, Stefon was suddenly a superstar. He found himself doing one interview after another. Companies wanted him to be their spokesperson. He advertised suits on the back of magazines. GEICO Insurance created an advertisement campaign around him and his "sticky hands." He was also featured in commercials for Pizza Hut and Bose audio equipment.

In April, the Pro Football Hall of Fame announced that they would display the cleats that Stefon wore during the Minneapolis Miracle.

EXTRA POINT

The Minneapolis Miracle won the NFL Play of the Year Award and the Best Moment ESPY Award from ESPN.

Despite being pulled in so many different directions, Stefon concentrated on his family. His brothers Mar'Sean

Stefon attended the ESPY Awards in 2018.

and Trevon had NFL aspirations of their own, and Stefon was in a position to help them accomplish their dreams. He spent time during the off-season working with his brothers to improve their football knowledge and skills. He showed them proper footwork, talked about what NFL coaches look for, and encouraged them to work hard and believe in themselves to succeed.

He also routinely beat them playing *Madden NFL* on the PlayStation 4.

The Vikings didn't wait for Stefon to finish out the final year of his 4-year contract. They negotiated a new deal to keep him in Minnesota at least until 2023.

In July of 2018, Stefon signed a 5-year contract worth $72 million, with a $15 million signing bonus. The deal made him one of the top 10 highest-paid wide receivers in the league.

The Vikings banked on Stefon's future. Stefon, on the other hand, thought about the past. His father, so many years ago, had asked him to take care of his mother and brothers. Stefon now had the means to do just that.

His mother was with him during the press conference, when the contract was announced to the media. Stefon became emotional when he spoke of the promise to his father. He was happy to be able to look after his family.

In September of 2018, Stefon appeared on a celebrity edition of *Family Feud*, a popular TV game show. His team made it to the final round. There, Stefon's answers were more than enough to win the game. In doing so, his team raised $25,000 for the Professional Athletes Foundation, a charity that helps former athletes with everything from education assistance to health care resources.

From there, Stefon turned his focus to his next goal: proving to the Minnesota Vikings that they were right to extend his contract.

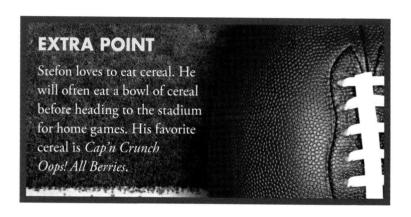

EXTRA POINT

Stefon loves to eat cereal. He will often eat a bowl of cereal before heading to the stadium for home games. His favorite cereal is *Cap'n Crunch Oops! All Berries*.

22

⟨⟨⟨⟨⟨ NEW QUARTERBACK ⟩⟩⟩⟩⟩

The Vikings didn't win the championship, but they had been close. If they could improve their play at a few positions, maybe 2018 would be their year.

Case Keenum had been spectacular in 2017, but the Vikings found a quarterback whom they believed would be even better: former Washington Redskins superstar Kirk Cousins. The Vikings signed him to a 3-year deal.

Minnesota began their season at home with a 24–16 victory over the San Francisco 49ers. Stefon caught 3 passes for 43 yards, including a 22-yard touchdown.

In Week 2, the Vikings traveled to Green Bay for an epic battle that ultimately left both teams feeling deflated. The Packers dominated through three quarters of play, gaining a 20–7 advantage.

In the opening minute of the fourth quarter, Stefon caught a short pass at the goal line and reached in for the score. The 3-yard play cut the lead to 20–14.

Green Bay answered by doing just what they needed to do. They milked 7 minutes off the clock on their way to a field goal. The score put the Vikings in a difficult position. With only 7:35 left in the game, their only hope was to score quickly.

The team called on Stefon, and he delivered. From the 25-yard line, Cousins dropped back to pass. He launched the ball 55 yards down the middle of the field. Despite being double-covered, Stefon hauled in the catch. He angled to his right and was tripped up by a defender—but not before he stumbled across the goal line.

After just 17 seconds of play, Minnesota was back in the game, trailing 23–21.

The Packers added two field goals to their lead, giving them an 8-point edge with just 1:45 to go.

Minnesota still had a chance. However, it looked as if the game was lost when Cousins threw an interception. But a controversial roughing the passer penalty gave the ball back to the Vikings.

This time, Cousins carved up the Packers defense. A 22-yard touchdown pass to Adam Thielen put the game within reach. But Minnesota needed to execute a 2-point conversion to tie.

With the ball placed at the 2-yard line, Stefon faked a route into the middle of the field, then he burst toward the back corner of the end zone. He was wide open, and Cousins lofted a pass to him. Stefon grabbed the football, tapped his toes in bounds, and tied the game at 29–29.

Minnesota had just scored 22 fourth-quarter points in a thrilling comeback. It should have been remembered as one of the greatest games in team history. But in overtime, the Vikings missed two field goals. The game ended in a tie that disappointed both teams.

Stefon finished with 128 yards on 9 receptions. His teammate Thielen gained 131 yards on 12 catches. The duo of receivers was being talked about as arguably the best tandem in the NFL.

The disappointing finish in Green Bay was followed by an even more disappointing performance. The heavily

Stefon and Adam Thielen are among the league's best wide receivers.

favored Vikings lost at home to the Buffalo Bills in a blowout, 27–6.

Stefon snagged 11 receptions for 123 yards against the Los Angeles Rams. While the Vikings offense exploded for 31 points, Minnesota's defense couldn't solve the Rams' passing attack. The team fell to Los Angeles, 38–31.

The Vikings started to get back on track a week later. They beat the Eagles, 23–21. They defeated Arizona by a count of 27–17. Then they routed the New York Jets, 37–17.

Their winning streak ended at the hands of the New Orleans Saints, who paid back the Minneapolis Miracle with a 30–20 victory. It was Stefon's most productive game in a month. He caught 10 passes for 119 yards and a touchdown.

A rib injury sidelined Stefon against Detroit. But the Vikings came away with a 24–9 victory, improving their record to 5–3–1.

EXTRA POINT

In 2018, Case Keenum moved on to the Denver Broncos. He started at quarterback for them all season.

23

1,000 YARDS

Stefon utilized a bye week to recover from his injury. Then he joined the team in Chicago to face the 6–3 Bears. Stefon caught 13 passes for 126 yards, but Chicago took the game, 25–20.

Green Bay came to U.S. Bank Stadium the following week. Stefon scored a touchdown on a 30-yard pass from Cousins. He finished the game with 8 catches for 77 yards in a 24–17 win.

But the up-and-down season swung back down again. Minnesota fell to the New England Patriots and then to the Seattle Seahawks.

With three games left in the regular season, Minnesota's record stood at 6–6–1. Their only hope of getting into the playoffs was to win their final three games.

Minnesota's star wide receivers both stood out in an otherwise mediocre season. Thielen was leading the team with 103 catches for 1,236 yards. Stefon had tallied 88 receptions for 915 yards.

In order to reach his first 100-catch, 1,000-yard regular season, Stefon would need to average just 4 receptions for 28 yards in the final three games.

It seemed like a sure thing.

The Vikings earned a much-needed win versus the Miami Dolphins in what might have been their best game of the year. They handily defeated the Dolphins, 41–17. Stefon caught 4 passes for 49 yards and a touchdown.

He only posted 2 receptions for 10 yards against the Detroit Lions. Still, the Vikings won again, 27–9.

The final contest on their schedule matched up the Vikings with the NFC North champions, the Chicago Bears. For Minnesota, the importance of the game was obvious. If they beat the Bears, they were in the playoffs. If they lost, the season was over.

There was a reason why the Bears had played to an 11–4 record. They were a really good team. It was clear from the beginning that the Vikings were overmatched. Chicago dominated, and Minnesota lost the game, 24–10.

The only good news was that Stefon caught 8 passes for 47 yards and a touchdown. It was enough to lift him into the 100/1,000 club. He finished the season with 102 receptions for 1,021 yards.

EXTRA POINT

Stefon seems to get better every year because he always wants to learn. He often contacts his coaches to ask what else he can do to improve.

24

⟨⟨⟨⟨⟨ BRIGHT FUTURE ⟩⟩⟩⟩⟩

Stefon has always been about family. The Minnesota Vikings became an extension of his own—and Stefon wanted his family to succeed. Just as he worked with his brothers to make their dreams come true, he also worked with the Vikings to do the same.

Stefon's brother Trevon was a member of the national championship team at the University of Alabama in 2017. He missed much of the 2018 season with a broken foot. So Trevon chose to stay for his senior year.

In April of 2019, Minnesota invited Mar'Sean Diggs to try out with the team. Stefon congratulated his brother but told him to keep his head down and do the work. Mar'Sean was not offered a contract, but he continued pursuing his NFL dream.

Stefon began working on more than football. During the off-season, he went back to the University of Maryland to earn his college degree in African American Studies, with a minor in Communications.

With a focus on family, on football, and on education, Stefon stayed busy. Yet he made time to get involved with charities and to help other people. He worked with Pillsbury United Communities to help children and families throughout the Minneapolis area. He made surprise visits to children's hospitals to spread comfort and joy where he could. He donated turkey dinners to families in need at Thanksgiving. He wore custom cleats to support the American Heart Association, in honor of his father. The list of people whom Stefon has helped is long, and it continues to grow.

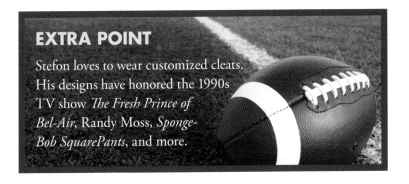

EXTRA POINT

Stefon loves to wear customized cleats. His designs have honored the 1990s TV show *The Fresh Prince of Bel-Air*, Randy Moss, *SpongeBob SquarePants*, and more.

On the field Stefon believes that he can do even more to help his team. With new offensive coaches and a new approach, Stefon is excited about the seasons to come. He hopes to help the Vikings earn their way back into the playoffs and bring an NFL championship to Minnesota.

EPILOGUE

A great play is never just a great play. Hours of practice go into every instant. Months of training are a piece of each moment. And, sometimes, a lifetime of effort boils down to just a few seconds of action.

So it was with the Miracle.

Keenum had done his job. Twenty-seven yards downfield, the football arrived—a little high but within reach. Stefon had to leap and extend his arms, but he snagged the football out of the air.

He came down on one foot. He turned and stumbled. He planted a hand on the ground to gain his balance, got up, and kept going.

The crowd's rumble became a sudden cheer, increasing in intensity as Stefon raced toward the end zone. The sound carried him until U.S. Bank Stadium erupted in a joyous, disbelieving roar.

Stefon Diggs held up the football. He dashed across the goal line and into the history books.

Sixty-one yards. Ten seconds.

Anything is possible.

ADAM THIELEN

Adam Thielen grew up in rural Minnesota. He dreamed of one day playing in the pros, but no one could imagine the path that awaited him. This is the story of Adam's rise from an unrecruited, undrafted small-town football player to one of the best wide receivers in professional sports.

JAMES CONNER

THE TRIUMPHS OF A FOOTBALL HERO

JAMES CONNER

BY LARRY SCHARDT

In high school, James Conner was an unblockable defensive end. When he got his chance at lead running back, he became one of the most exciting players in the country. But after a severe injury and a cancer diagnosis, his future in football was in jeopardy.

PHILLIP LINDSAY

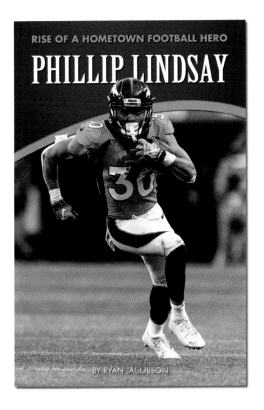

Growing up in Denver, Phillip Lindsay experienced injury, rejection, and disappointment, but the young running back never gave up. This is a story of determination and perseverance. It is proof that anything is possible with hard work and a winning attitude.

YOU'RE THE MAIN CHARACTER.
YOU MAKE THE CHOICES.
CHOOSE TO WIN!

Enjoy this clever twist to sports-themed children's fiction. In each interactive story, the reader becomes the main character and makes choices that affect what happens next. Points are awarded for different choices, which readers use later in the book to upgrade their skills.

SOURCES

"2015 NFL Draft: Recap of Second and Third Round Picks in Day 2."
NBC Sports (nbcsports.com). May 1, 2015.

Aaron, John. "Area HS Players Set to Take National Football Stage."
WTOP: Washington's Top News (wtop.com). January 5, 2012.

Abruzzese, David. "Stefon Diggs Strikes an Official During Pregame
Scuffle." Onward State (onwardstate.com). November 3, 2014.

All-American Bowl. "2012 U.S. Army All-American Bowl." YouTube
(youtube.com). Accessed June 27, 2019.

"All-WCAC Football Team." DC-Washington Catholic Athletic
Conference (79224.digitalsports.com). November 20, 2008.

American Heart Association News. "Minnesota Vikings Star
Receiver Stefon Diggs Honors Father, Grandmother with Custom
Cleats." American Heart Association (newsarchive.heart.org).
Accessed July 5, 2019.

AP. "Injury-Ravaged Vikings Get WR Stefon Diggs Back at Practice."
USA Today (usatoday.com). November 28, 2016.

"Aron Diggs Obituary." *The Washington Post*
(legacy.com/obituaries/washingtonpost). Accessed May 5, 2019.

Auerbach, Nicole. "Whether Family or Football, Maryland's Stefon
Diggs Cherishes What Can Be Lost." *USA Today* (usatoday.com).
August 13, 2014.

Axelrod, Ben. "Ohio State Football: What Could Have Been if Urban
Meyer Had Landed Stefon Diggs." Bleacher Report (bleacherreport.com).
October 2, 2014.

Barker, Jeff. *The Baltimore Sun* (baltimoresun.com).
- "Stefon Diggs Looking Forward to Catching Passes from Just One
  QB This Year." August 29, 2013.
- "For Diggs Brothers, Departed Father Serves as Motivation."
  August 4, 2013.

Barr, Josh. "WCAC Championship: Good Counsel Clinches First Undefeated Season in School History with 42–0 Victory over Gonzaga." *The Washington Post* (washingtonpost.com). November 19, 2011.

Bekore, Lynda. "Underclassmen and the NFL Draft: To Declare or Not to Declare?" Huffpost (huffpost.com). December 6, 2017.

Boyd, Jimmy. "Complete History of the Super Bowl Curse & Host City." Boyd's Bets (boydsbets.com). January 21, 2019.

Brady, James. "NFL Draft 2015: Pick-by-Pick Results." SB Nation (sbnation.com). May 2, 2015.

Broome, Anthony. 247 Sports (247sports.com).
- "Stefon Diggs Leaves Game vs. Bears with Groin Injury." October 9, 2017.
- "Stefon Diggs Shares 5 Favorite Childhood Movies." July 19, 2017.

Carlson, Adam. "Stefon Diggs' Cleats Headed to the Pro Football Hall of Fame." The Viking Age (thevikingage.com). April 18, 2018.

Casagrande, Michael. "How NFL Star Stefon Diggs Helps Alabama DB Younger Brother." Alabama Local News (al.com). May 2, 2019.

Clements, Ron. "Maryland Pro Day Standout Stefon Diggs Loves Football 'Too Much.'" Sporting News (sportingnews.com). April 2, 2015.

Coleman, Michael. "Vikings' Stefon Diggs Exuberant over TD Catch—too Exuberant." *Pioneer Press* (twincities.com). November 12, 2017.

"Congestive Heart Failure (CHF)." Healthline (healthline.com). Accessed May 26, 2019.

Coyer, Nicholas. "Falling from Grace: The Story of the 2016 Minnesota Vikings." The Viking Age (thevikingage.com). December 26, 2016.

Craig, Mark. "Vikings Give Defensive Back Mar'Sean Diggs a Look During Rookie Camp." *StarTribune* (startribune.com). May 5, 2019.

Cronin, Courtney. "Stefon Diggs Suffered Rib Injury vs. Saints, Hasn't Practiced This Week." ESPN (espn.com). November 1, 2018.

Davenport, Gary. "Why Maryland's Stefon Diggs Could Be the Biggest WR Steal of the 2015 NFL Draft." Bleacher Report (bleacherreport.com). March 30, 2015.

"DeMatha Stags Win 2008 WCAC Football Championship!" The Chronicles of Six (dicooper.wordpress.com). Accessed July 2, 2019.

"Diamondback Terrapin (Malaclemys Terrapin)." Savannah River Ecology Laboratory: University of Georgia (srelherp.uga.edu). Accessed May 29, 2019.

Diggs, Stefon. "Inside My Second Season." *The Players Tribune* (theplayerstribune.com). December 23, 2016.

Dunn, Katherine. "Jennings Named Gatorade Maryland Football Player of the Year." *The Baltimore Sun* (baltimoresun.com). December 2, 2010.

Ekstrom, Sam. "'My Pops Left Me a Message;' How the Loss of His Father Drove Stefon Diggs." 92 KQRS Radio (92kqrs.com). August 1, 2018.

Ellis, Zac. "Maryland Receivers Stefon Diggs, Deon Long Out for Season with Leg Injuries." *Sports Illustrated* (si.com). October 19, 2013.

Ermann, Jeff. "How Did So Many NFL Teams Miss on Diggs?" 247 Sports (247sports.com). September 19, 2016.

ESPN (espn.com).
- "Terrapins 2018 Roster." Accessed June 14, 2019.
- "Vikings Lose Bridgewater, Beat Rams 21–18 in OT." November 8, 2015.
- Standford vs. Maryland. December 30, 2014.
- Maryland vs. Penn State. November 1, 2014.
- Maryland vs. Wisconsin. October 25, 2014.
- Iowa vs. Maryland. October 18, 2014.
- Ohio State vs Maryland. October 4, 2014.
- Maryland vs. Indiana. September 27, 2014.
- West Virginia vs. Maryland. September 13, 2014.
- James Madison vs. Maryland. August 30, 2014.
- Maryland vs. Wake Forest. October 19, 2013.
- Maryland vs. Connecticut. September 14, 2013.
- Georgia Tech vs. Maryland. November 3, 2012.
- Wake Forest vs. Maryland. October 6, 2012.
- William & Mary vs. Maryland. September 1, 2012.

"Estimated Probability of Competing in Professional Athletics." NCAA (ncaa.org). Accessed May 19, 2019.

Gallen, Daniel. "Former Maryland Star Stefon Diggs Named to NFL All-Rookie Team." *Carroll County Times* (carrollcountytimes.com). January 20, 2016.

Garland, Ryan. "Stefon Diggs' Mark on Maryland Goes Beyond Stats." Terrapin Station MD (terrapinstationmd.com). Accessed June 9, 2019.

Gates, Christopher. Daily Norseman (dailynorseman.com).
- "Stefon Diggs Becomes Fastest to 200 Catches in Vikings' History." January 1, 2018.
- "Stefon Diggs Raised a Few Eyebrows with a Celebrity Family Feud Answer." September 18, 2018.

Geary, Molly. "Edsall Says Diggs 'Took a Ding' in WVU Game." Testudo Times (testudotimes.com). October 17, 2013.

Ginsburg, David. "College Football: Maryland Rallies Past Iowa, 38–31." *Telegraph Herald* (telegraphherald.com). October 18, 2014.

Goessling, Ben. ESPN (espn.com).
- "Stefon Diggs Says Groin Injury Bothered Him for Most of 2016." June 1, 2017.
- "Teddy Bridgewater Injury Casts Doubts on Vikings' Playoff Chances." September 6, 2016.
- "Vikings QB Teddy Bridgewater Dislocates Knee, Tears ACL in Drill." August 31, 2016.

Goessling, Ben. "Vikings Receiver Stefon Diggs Comfortable as a Nonconformist." *StarTribune* (startribune.com). October 27, 2018.

Goldstein, Jared. "Who's the Best Wide Receiver in Maryland Football History?" Testudo Times (testudotimes.com). June 20, 2017.

Goodbread, Chase. "2015 NFL Draft to Be Held April 30–May 2." NFL.com (nfl.com). October 2, 2014.

Harris, Chris. "Wide Receiver Stefon Diggs—with the Famous Side Part—Is Back from Injury and Shares His Barber." The Undefeated (theundefeated.com). October 31, 2017.

Hinnen, Jerry. "Maryland WRs Stefon Diggs, Deon Long Both Out for Season." CBS Sports (cbssports.com). October 20, 2013.

huntva. "2011 Good Counsel Defeats Manatee in 2 Overtimes Thriller Highlights." YouTube (youtube.com). September 3, 2011.

Jason, Christopher. "Ohio State–Maryland 2014: Taking a Closer Look at Stefon Diggs." Land-Grant Holy Land (landgrantholyland.com). October 3, 2014.

Kirk, Jason. "Perry Hills Injury: ACL Injury Ends Maryland Starting QB's Year." SB Nation (sbnation.com). October 22, 2012.

Lund, Ryan. "Vikings' Stefon Diggs Ranks Among Rookie Greats Through Four Games." FOX Sports (foxsports.com). November 5, 2015.

Madden, Brian. "Keenum Explains X's & O's of the 'Minneapolis Miracle' with Broncos Fans." 4 CBS Denver (denver.cbslocal.com). June 21, 2018.

Martin, Daniel. NBC Sports (nbcsports.com).
- "Through 4 Games, Stefon Diggs Already Sets NFL Record." November 6, 2015.
- "4 Reasons Why Stefon Diggs Was Smart to Head to the NFL." October 19, 2015.
- "Former Maryland Star Diggs Declared Inactive Again." September 27, 2015.
- "Minnesota Vikings Draft Maryland's Stefon Diggs." May 2, 2015.

Martinez, Jose. "Vikings Player Stefon Diggs Buys Custom $15,000 Starbucks Chain." Complex Media (complex.com). September 12, 2018.

MaxPreps (maxpreps.com).
- "Stefon Diggs' Football Stats." Accessed July 2, 2019.
- "Our Lady of Good Counsel 2011 Football Schedule." Accessed June 10, 2019.
- "Our Lady of Good Counsel 2010 Football Schedule." Accessed July 2, 2019.
- DeMatha vs. Our Lady of Good Counsel. October 9, 2009.
- Gilman vs. Our Lady of Good Counsel. September 17, 2009.
- "Our Lady of Good Counsel 2009 Football Schedule." Accessed July 2, 2019.
- "Our Lady of Good Counsel 2008 Football Schedule." Accessed July 2, 2019.

McAtee, Riley. "The Vikings Just Bet Big on the Potential of Stefon Diggs." The Ringer (theringer.com). July 31, 2018.

McFadden, Kyle. "Minneapolis Miracle Man: Stefon Diggs Finally Gets His Moment on the National Stage." KFadd (kfadd.com). January 20, 2018.

"Md. Star Takes Combine MVP." Rivals (rivals.com). January 12, 2011.

"Medial and Lateral Meniscus Tears." Cedars-Sinai.org (cedars-sinai.org). Accessed June 18, 2019.

Mickle, Shane. "4 Things to Know About Vikings Wide Receiver Stefon Diggs." Clutch Points (clutchpoints.com). June 17, 2019.

Montes, Sebastian. "Chiefs Claim Their First State Title." Patch (patch.com). December 28, 2011.

Myerberg, Paul. *USA Today* (usatoday.com).
- "Big Ten Suspends Maryland's Stefon Diggs, Reprimands Coach." November 3, 2014.
- "Maryland's Next Up at QB: A True Freshman Linebacker." October 29, 2012.

Neiner, Zack. "'Disrespectful' Handshake Steals Spotlight in Maryland–Penn State Game." *Daily Collegian* (collegian.psu.edu). November 1, 2014.

Nelson, Joe. "18 Wide Receivers Were Drafted Ahead of Stefon Diggs in 2015." Bring Me the News (bringmethenews.com). August 12, 2018.

NFL. "Home Radio Broadcasters Freak Out on Stefon Diggs Walk-Off Minneapolis Miracle TD!" YouTube (youtube.com). January 15, 2018.

NFL.com (nfl.com).
- "Stefon Diggs Plays with Daughter During Pregame." Accessed June 16, 2019.
- Minnesota Vikings 2018 Schedule. Accessed May 31, 2019.
- Minnesota Vikings 2017 Schedule. Accessed May 31, 2019.
- Minnesota Vikings 2016 Schedule. Accessed May 28, 2019.
- Minnesota Vikings 2015 Schedule. Accessed May 28, 2019.
- Green Bay Packers 2015 Schedule. Accessed June 5, 2019.

"NFL Game Center." NFL.com (nfl.com).
- Chicago vs. Minnesota. December 30, 2018.
- Green Bay vs. Minnesota. November 25, 2018.
- Minnesota vs. Chicago. November 18, 2018.
- Minnesota vs. Green Bay. September 16, 2018.
- San Francisco vs. Minnesota. September 9, 2018.
- New Orleans vs. Minnesota. January 14, 2018.
- Minnesota vs. Washington. November 12, 2017.
- New Orleans vs. Minnesota. September 11, 2017.

- Green Bay vs. Minnesota. September 18, 2016.
- Seattle vs. Minnesota. January 10, 2016.
- Minnesota vs. Green Bay. January 3, 2016.
- Chicago vs. Minnesota. December 20, 2015.
- Minnesota vs. Oakland. November 15, 2015.
- Minnesota vs. Chicago. November 1, 2015.
- Minnesota vs. Detroit. October 25, 2015.
- Minnesota vs. Denver. October 4, 2015.
- Minnesota vs. Tennessee. September 3, 2015.
- Minnesota vs. Dallas. August 29, 2015.
- Tampa Bay vs. Minnesota. August 15, 2015.
- Pittsburgh vs. Minnesota. August 9, 2015.

"NFL Names 'Minneapolis Miracle' Play of the Year." WCCO 4 News (minnesota.cbslocal.com). February 3, 2018.

"NFL Players" (nfl.com).
- "Adam Thielen." Accessed May 28, 2019.
- "Stefon Diggs." Accessed May 28, 2019.

Olojede, Zion. "Stefon Diggs Is More Than the Guy with the Crazy Custom Cleats." Complex (complex.com). September 11, 2017.

Olson, Nick. "Vikings' Stefon Diggs' Four-Game, 419-yard Breakout Rookie Performance." NFLBreakdowns (nflbreakdowns.com). November 4, 2015.

Patra, Kevin. NFL (nfl.com).
- "Vikings WR Stefon Diggs Signs Five-Year Extension." July 31, 2018.
- "Stefon Diggs Ruled Out for Vikings vs. Lions." November 24, 2016.

Pell, Samantha. "Before NFL Success with Vikings, Stefon Diggs Was Impossible to Stop in High School." *The Washington Post* (washingtonpost.com). January 11, 2018.

Peters, Craig. "Vikings 'Miracle' Play Wins ESPY Award." Minnesota Vikings (vikings.com). July 18, 2018.

Pimpo Jr., Stephen. "Vikings Hero Stefon Diggs Was Making Plays in Maryland Before Becoming an NFL Star." WJLA7 News (wjla.com). January 15, 2018.

Prewitt, Alex. "Maryland's Stefon Diggs, Wes Brown Ruled Out for Clemson Game with Ankle Injuries." *The Washington Post* (washingtonpost.com). November 8, 2012.

Pro Football Reference (pro-football-reference.com).
- "2016 Minnesota Vikings Injuries." Accessed June 22, 2019.
- "Stefon Diggs." Accessed May 5, 2019.

Rapaport, Daniel. "Sam Bradford Says His Knee Injury Not from Contact." *Sports Illustrated* (si.com). September 20, 2017.

"Records." Our Lady of Good Counsel Football Team (goodcounselfootball.com). Accessed June 22, 2019.

Riley, Stephen D. "A Streak of Their Own: Good Counsel Captures Second Straight Title with 42–3 Win Over DeMatha." *The Afro-American* (afro.com). November 21, 2010.

Ross, Garrett. "Maryland Defeats Penn State, 20–19; Apologizes for No Handshakes." Daily Collegian (collegian.psu.edu). November 1, 2014.

Sallee, Barrett. "2019 NFL Draft: Record Number of College Football Players Enter with Eligibility Remaining." CBS Sports (cbssports.com). January 18, 2019.

Seifert, Kevin. "Inside the Play That Saved the Vikings' Season—and Crushed the Saints." ESPN (espn.com). January 14, 2018.

Sessler, Marc. NFL.com (nfl.com).
- "Dalvin Cook Suffers Knee Injury in Loss to Lions." October 1, 2017.
- "Stefon Diggs Stealing the Show for Vikings' Air Attack." November 2, 2015.

Shealer, Sheldon. "Young's Play Ends Old Run of Results." ESPN (espn.com). November 22, 2009.

Silverstein, Adam. "Stefon Diggs Spurns Florida, Commits to Maryland." Only Gators (onlygators.com). February 10, 2012.

"Stefon Diggs." Sports Reference: College Football (sports-reference.com). Accessed May 29, 2019.

"Stefon Diggs Bio, Age, Height, Weight, Brother, Family, Other Facts." Heightline (heightline.com). Accessed May 5, 2019.

"Stefon Diggs' Family: 5 Fast Facts You Need to Know." Heavy (heavy.com). January 21, 2018.

"Stefon Diggs, Good Counsel, Wide Receiver." 247 Sports (247sports.com). Accessed June 9, 2019.

"Stefon Diggs Helps Deliver Turkeys in Frogtown." Minnesota Vikings (vikings.com). November 21, 2018.

"Stefon Diggs' Mother Stephanie Diggs." Fabwags (Fabwags.com). Accessed on May 7, 2019.

"Stefon Diggs Track & Field Bio." Athletic.net (athletic.net). Accessed June 23, 2019.

"Stefon Diggs TV Commercial Ads." iSpot.TV (ispot.tv). Accessed June 30, 2019.

Stephenson, Creg. "Maryland WR Suspended, School Fined for Pre-Game Scuffle, Handshake Incident Vs. Penn State." Alabama Local News (al.com). November 3, 2014.

Stubbs, Roman. "Stefon Diggs Keeps Memories of Father in Moving on From Injury and Toward Stardom." *The Washington Post* (washingtonpost.com). August 29, 2014.

Tenorio, Paul. "Stefon Diggs Commits to Maryland, Ending Speculation over Plans of the Good Counsel Star." *The Washington Post* (washingtonpost.com). February 10, 2012.

Tomasson, Chris. *Pioneer Press* (twincities.com).
- "Tryout Player Mar'Sean Diggs Hoping to Join Brother Stefon on Vikings." May 3, 2019.
- "Vikings' Stefon Diggs Returns to Where It All Started." November 11, 2016.
- "Vikings WR Stefon Diggs Out Against Texans with Groin Injury." October 9, 2016.
- "Diggs Entertaining Family Today." November 21, 2015.

Trahan, Kevin and Luke Zimmermann. "Stefon Diggs Looking Forward to Facing Ohio State, Urban Meyer." Land-Grant Holy Land (landgrantholyland.com). July 29, 2014.

Trotter, Jim. "Saints–Vikings Rematch: Stefon Diggs Talks 'Minneapolis Miracle.'" NFL.com (nfl.com). October 24, 2018.

TYT Sports. "Stefon Diggs' Emotional Response to His New Contract." YouTube (www.youtube.com). August 1, 2018.

University of Maryland (umterps.com).
- "2014 Football Roster: Stefon Diggs." Accessed May 29, 2019.
- "2014 Football Schedule." Accessed June 5, 2019.
- Maryland vs. Wake Forest. October 19, 2013.
- "2013 Football Schedule." Accessed June 5, 2019.
- "2012 Football Schedule." Accessed May 29, 2019.

Van Bibber, Ryan. "How . . . Did the Vikings Pull off the 'Minnesota Miracle?'" SB Nation (sbnation.com). January 21, 2018.

Verderame, Matt. "Stefon Diggs Is Talented on and off the Field." Fansided (fansided.com). Accessed July 5, 2019.

"Vikings Place Adrian Peterson (Meniscus) on Injured Reserve." *Sports Illustrated* (si.com). September 21, 2016.

Volk, Pete. "C.J. Brown Injured Against Florida State." Testudo Times (testudotimes.com). October 5, 2013.

Wasserman, Ari. "'I Can Relate to a Guy Who Stays Home': Maryland WR Stefon Diggs, a Former Ohio State Target, Uniquely Understands LeBron James." Cleveland.com (cleveland.com). October 1, 2014.

Weathersby, Edwin. "Stefon Diggs to Maryland: The Top 5 Reasons Why He Picked the Terps." Bleacher Report (bleacherreport.com). February 22, 2012.

Wells, Adam. "Stefon Diggs Inactive vs. Lions with Rib Injury." Bleacher Report (bleacherreport.com). November 4, 2018.

Whittington, Grant. "Maryland's Stefon Diggs Could Break 20 Records This Year." Testudo Times (testudotimes.com). July 21, 2014.

"Who We Are." Professional Athletes Foundation (yourpaf.com). Accessed June 30, 2019.

Wilkerson, William. "Diggs Standing Out on and off Field." ESPN (espn.com). January 6, 2012.

Williams, Preston. "Remembering the Most Significant Stories from This Past School Year." *The Washington Post* (pressreader.com). June 16, 2010.

Wiltfong, Steve. "The Evolution of Stefon Diggs." 247 Sports (247sports.com). September 25, 2011.

Yotter, Tim. "Surviving Injury Part of Diggs' Dossier." 247 Sports (247sports.com). May 2, 2015.

Young, Lindsey. "Stefon Diggs Gives Back Through Gaming." Minnesota Vikings (vikings.com). December 18, 2018.

Zenitz, Matt. *Baltimore Sun* (baltimoresun.com).
- "Stefon Diggs Tweets about Maryland Football's Hometown 'Movement'." December 15, 2014.
- "Terps Star Stefon Diggs Lacerated Kidney Against Penn State, Sources Say." November 10, 2014.

Zinski, Dan. "Stefon Diggs Is Active for the Vikings." The Viking Age (thevikingage.com). October 4, 2015.

PHOTOGRAPHY CREDITS

ABOUT THE AUTHOR

Doug Olson, Jr., holds a degree in journalism from the University of Minnesota. He has contributed several pieces of fiction and nonfiction to various publications, including some comic book work.

A storyteller by nature, Doug spent countless hours regaling neighborhood kids with tales of ghosts, super-heroes, and *The Six-Million Dollar Man* "fan fiction," before such a thing existed. He has continued his love of wordsmithing throughout his life, even when he knows it may never be seen by another human being.

Doug enjoys creating, brainstorming with friends, playing *World of Warcraft*, and, of course, following his beloved Minnesota Vikings. He lives in the Minneapolis area with his wife, two children, and four small fur-babies.